Beyond OK

A CEO's Journey Through Burnout To Mental Wellness

John Ainsworth & Christine Chinyama

Copyright © 2025 John Ainsworth & Christine Chinyama
All rights reserved.

No part of this publication may be reproduced, stored in a retrieval system, or transmitted in any form or by any means—electronic, mechanical, photocopying, recording, or otherwise—without the prior written permission of the copyright owner, except in the case of brief quotations embodied in critical articles or reviews.

Contents

Dedication i
About This Book ii
About the Authors iii
Foreword 1
Preface 4
Important Notice to Readers 6
Medical Disclaimer 7
Author Relationship Disclosure 8
Privacy Notice 9
Introduction The Breaking Point 10
Chapter 1 The Human Behind the Executive Mask - Learning from the Butterfly 17
Chapter 2 When Your Brain Betrays You - Understanding Trauma and Fear 40
Chapter 3 The Self-Sabotage Trap – 55
Chapter 4 The Courage to Be Vulnerable – 71
Chapter 5 Breaking Free from Co-Dependency – Reclaiming Your Power 94
Chapter 6 Taming the Mind's Predictions - Overcoming Anxious Thoughts and Blocking Beliefs 112
Chapter 7 Control the Controllables - Finding Peace in Uncertainty 131
Chapter 8 The Power of Now - Living in the Present Moment .. 148
Chapter 9 Winning in Your Mind First - The Mental Game of Success 167
Chapter 10 What if OK Wasn't OK? 187

Dedication

For Megan and Jessica, the greatest part of my life.

My love for you has no limits. I am so proud of you both.

Dad

To my husband and children, thank you for your unwavering support over the years.

Christine

About This Book

This book draws on my personal experiences as a senior executive. While the emotions, challenges, and insights are authentically mine, some details have been generalised or modified to protect confidentiality and focus on universal lessons rather than specific organisations or individuals.

My purpose is not to criticise any particular company or person, but to share what I learned about mental health, leadership, and resilience in the hope it helps others facing similar challenges. The book serves an educational purpose, combining personal narrative with clinical CBT insights.

The organisational challenges I describe are common across many businesses and industries. If you recognise yourself or others in these pages, please know that my intent is to illuminate universal leadership challenges and mental health struggles, not to judge or disparage anyone. We're all doing our best with the tools and understanding we have at the time.

About the Authors

John Ainsworth

John Ainsworth is a former CEO of a regulated company, where he led major organisational change under intense pressure and scrutiny. With over two decades of experience in high-stakes leadership roles, John reached the top of his profession—only to find himself facing an internal crisis that success couldn't shield him from.

His personal experience of burnout and mental health breakdown became the catalyst for a powerful journey of self-discovery, recovery, and transformation. Now an entrepreneur, speaker, and advocate for mental wellness in leadership, John draws on both his professional expertise and deeply personal story to help others thrive—not just survive—in demanding careers.

In *Beyond OK*, John offers a rare, honest account of what it truly means to lead while struggling inside, and how vulnerability, self-awareness, and psychological tools can help leaders reclaim their health and authenticity. His mission is simple but profound: to break the silence around executive mental health and to show that growth is possible—even after the breaking point.

Christine Chinyama

Postgraduate PGDip, BSc (Hons) BABCP Accredited Cognitive Behavioural Therapist

Christine is a full accredited Cognitive Behavioural Therapist with 10 years of experience supporting adults and young people with a wide range of mental health challenge. She holds a post graduate diploma in CBT Buckinghamshire New University and is accredited with British Association for Behavioural and Cognitive Psychotherapies (BABCP).

Christine specialises in working with individuals experiencing anxiety, depression, panic disorder, social anxiety and obsessive-compulsive disorder (OCD) she also support clients through work related stress, and trauma.

Over the years she has worked in both NHS IAPT and private settings, bringing a depth of experience and cultural sensitivity to her work. Her approach is warm, collaborative, and evidence based. Christine believes in empowering clients to understand the connections between their thoughts, feelings and behaviour, and to build practical skills that support long term well-being. She integrates mindfulness, compassion -focused, person-centred strategies when appropriate, tailoring therapy to each individual needs.

Outside of clinical work, Christine enjoys speaking about mental health in churches, spending time in nature. She currently offers sessions online.

First published in 2025 by Amazon

Foreword

Hello,

My name is Frank Bruno. I was a boxer who, over a period of time, reached the heights of becoming a World Champion. No one can take that away from me. However, when I go shopping, I am just a normal person. After boxing, I now talk about my life in boxing. In 2003, everything got on top of me. My family went as a result of a failed marriage, and I was rattling around in a large house. My brain, and in turn my mental health, said "enough is enough", and I was sectioned. It was a high-profile "section" with helicopters and news crews flying over my house, camera crews outside my house, and enough police for anybody to think I had committed the most awful crimes. My world collapsed. This has happened again a few times. However, I can now read the signs, and so can my family and management team. I now talk about mental health, and through my charity, my team tries to educate and advise people who have mental health issues. The subject of mental health, especially my own, was swept under the carpet until my manager, Dave Davies, convinced me to talk to a newspaper about my experiences and tell the world, "It's okay to say you are not okay", and ask for some help. My team and I have gone through this book and certain sections stood out for me:

Overcoming the Fear of Vulnerability

Breaking Free from Co-Dependency - Reclaiming Your Power

The Butterfly Comparisons to Life

I was reminded of one of my visits for a mental health talk with a famous Formula 1 team, where the immense pressure to make their car faster by 1 second was on the shoulders of a number of people, especially the senior management team. This book, to me, is like a car maintenance book for the brain and your mental health. It is packed full of advice and little exercises. My advice would be to read it slowly over a period of time, take in the advice, read it again, and act on the advice. John Ainsworth has risen to the top of his chosen profession, and suddenly, the mental health issues appeared, sometimes slowly, sometimes over a period of time, without too much attention being given to the symptoms. We live and work in a fast-paced world that does not limit itself to 5 days a week, 9-5. Children are increasingly showing signs of mental health issues at an early age. This book, no, let's call it a manual, needs to be read not only by those with existing mental health issues but also by those on the bottom rung of their career choice to help them guide their brain around potential issues as they climb the ladder.

I wish I had had this manual as I was growing up and progressing through my boxing career. We tend to focus on physical health, and I have always been an advocate for fitness and wellbeing, but the mind requires care and attention too. My hope is that this book will support you on your own journey, while also equipping you to guide others, as mental health challenges can affect family, friends, and colleagues alike. Read it with openness, take from it what you can, and use those insights not only to strengthen yourself but also to help those around you.

Finally, I love one of the statements near the end of the book:

"Remember this: you are not just OK. You are capable of extraordinary things. You deserve more than just getting by. You have the power to create a life of meaning, purpose, and authentic success. The choice, as always, is yours. What will you choose?"

Read it and use what you glean from the book to help other people and, of course, yourself. Most of all, look after yourself!

Regards,

Frank

The Frank Bruno Foundation

[www.thefrankbrunofoundation.co.uk]

(http://www.thefrankbrunofoundation.co.uk)

Frank's website for his history, appearances, gifts, and memorabilia: [www.frankbruno.co.uk]

(http://www.frankbruno.co.uk)

Preface

What happens when a successful CEO's mind becomes his greatest enemy?

John thought he had everything under control. Running a multi-million pound business, he projected strength and confidence to the world. But lying on a sun lounger in Thailand, tears streaming down his face, he realised the truth: he couldn't face returning to his executive role. His body and mind were screaming a single word: *ENOUGH*.

Beyond OK is the raw, honest story of one CEO's journey from breakdown to breakthrough—and the practical tools that can save your career, your relationships, and potentially your life.

Written with CBT therapist Christine, this isn't just another business memoir. It's a survival guide for executives who've discovered that success without mental wellness is just a beautifully decorated prison. Through the metaphor of the butterfly's transformation, John shares how the darkest period of his life became the catalyst for profound change.

Inside, you'll discover:

- Why the qualities that drive success can also destroy you
- How to recognise and interrupt self-sabotage patterns
- The neuroscience behind executive burnout and trauma
- CBT techniques specifically adapted for high-pressure leadership
- How vulnerability becomes your greatest leadership strength

- Tools for managing anxious predictions and limiting beliefs
- The art of controlling what you can whilst releasing what you can't

This book bridges the gap between clinical mental health resources and real-world executive challenges. It's for leaders who are tired of pretending they're "fine" when they're not, and ready to discover that their breakdown might actually be their breakthrough.

Because sometimes "OK" isn't OK—and that's exactly where transformation begins.

John Ainsworth is a former CEO who led organisational transformation in a UK business. Christine Chinyama is a CBT therapist specialising in mental health. Together, they've created the definitive resource for leaders navigating burnout and seeking authentic success.

Important Notice to Readers

This book is intended for informational and educational purposes only and is not a substitute for professional medical advice, diagnosis, or treatment. The content provided herein represents the personal experiences and observations of the authors and should not be considered medical or therapeutic advice.

Medical Disclaimer

The strategies, techniques, and insights shared in this book are based on personal experience and general research, not specific medical training. If you are experiencing mental health challenges, suicidal thoughts, or psychological distress, please seek immediate professional help from a qualified healthcare provider, licensed therapist, or mental health professional. Always consult with your GP or other qualified healthcare provider before making any changes to your mental health treatment or beginning any new practices described in this book.

The authors and publisher disclaim any liability for any adverse effects resulting from the use or application of the information contained in this book. Individual results may vary, and what worked for the authors may not be appropriate or effective for every reader.

Author Relationship Disclosure

This book represents a collaboration between John Ainsworth, who shares his personal journey through executive burnout and mental health recovery, and Christine Chinyama, a qualified Cognitive Behavioural Therapist. The authors acknowledge their previous therapeutic relationship, wherein Christine provided professional CBT services to John during his recovery process.

The therapeutic techniques and insights shared in this book are presented in an educational context and do not constitute a continuation of any therapeutic relationship. Readers should understand that the professional therapeutic relationship that previously existed between the authors has been appropriately concluded, and this collaboration exists solely for educational and informational purposes.

Crisis Resources

If you are in crisis or experiencing thoughts of self-harm, please contact:

- Emergency Services: 999
- Samaritans: 116 123 (free from any phone)
- NHS 111 for non-emergency medical advice
- Your local GP or A&E department

Privacy Notice

All personal details and case examples shared in this book have been anonymised or used with explicit consent. Some identifying details have been changed to protect privacy whilst maintaining the integrity of the experiences described.

By reading this book, you acknowledge that you understand and accept these disclaimers and agree to use the information responsibly.

Introduction
The Breaking Point

I am lying on a sun lounger in Thailand, trying to control my racing mind. All the thoughts seem to be negative and whatever I try doesn't seem to let me be at peace.

I should be relaxing and enjoying myself, fabulous weather, wonderful food and a break from what has been a crazy last year at work.

I have done so little that I planned on this trip. My body is tired, my mind is alive 24 hours a day and I battle to sleep and rest.

I awake on my final morning and as I do not need to leave the hotel until midday, I head to the pool and a sun lounger to catch the last bit of sun.

That's when it happens.

I don't feel right. Within minutes, I became completely overwhelmed. I'm not sobbing dramatically, but tears flow down my face in steady streams. Embarrassed, I retreat to my hotel room, asking myself the question that would change everything: *Why am I crying?*

The answer comes quickly, though I initially resist it: I don't want to go home.

I argue with myself. *Of course, you want to go home—you'll see your two beautiful daughters for the first time in two weeks.* But as I dig deeper, searching for the real reason behind my tears, the truth emerges with startling clarity: I can't face going back to work. My body and mind are screaming a single word: *ENOUGH!*

On my flight home, I had what I can only describe as a panic attack, which was a horrendous feeling. The feeling of claustrophobia when 30,000 feet in the air and you are travelling on your own is terrifying. I tried to control my breathing, which was exceptionally shallow, although I felt like I was gasping for breath. Eventually, we landed and I was able to leave the aircraft. Then, when I left the airport to head to my car, I just sat on a wall and cried.

How had it come to this? What should I do?

After returning home, I physically couldn't return to work. I sought help from my GP, who was brilliant—understanding, a great listener, and someone who truly did his profession proud. He explained that I was experiencing a depressive traumatic reaction due to prolonged stress. What disturbed me most was learning that this could have long-term impacts if I didn't seek proper help and support. It could even lead to Post-Traumatic Stress Disorder (PTSD).

Being caught in this vicious cycle of depressive symptoms was overwhelming. I had always believed myself to be in control, capable of facing any adversity. Yet this time it was my own mind turning against me. I began to anticipate the worst possible outcomes in my work situation, and it felt as though I was losing my strength and sense of control entirely.

This book is the story of my journey back from that breaking point—and the lessons I learnt that can help other high-achievers who find themselves in similar situations.

Why I'm Sharing My Story

I am sharing this deeply personal experience because I've learnt something crucial: the very qualities that drive us to success—perfectionism, relentless drive, the need to be strong for others—can also destroy us if left unchecked. As leaders, we're conditioned to project strength, to have all the answers, to never show weakness. But this conditioning can become a prison.

Throughout my career, I reached heights I never imagined possible when I left school at 16. Becoming CEO of a multi-million pound business exceeded every expectation I had for myself. Yet my hardest challenge was never external—it was always the thoughts I wrestled with, the worries that kept me awake, and the insecurities that lay beneath my outwardly confident exterior.

I've since learnt that this internal struggle has a name: anticipatory and objectless fear. More importantly, I've discovered how to manage and overcome it.

What Makes This Book Different

I've read countless books on mental health, listened to hundreds of hours of podcasts, and consumed every piece of content I could find on overcoming anxiety and depression. Whilst much of it was helpful, something vital was always missing: the real-world application to high-pressure business environments.

Most mental health resources are written by therapists and academics who, whilst expert in their fields, haven't walked in the shoes of someone running a complex business whilst battling their own mind. They haven't experienced the unique pressures of navigating frequent senior leadership changes, each requiring you to re-establish credibility and re-prove your capability.

This book bridges that gap. It combines professional psychological insights with lived experience from the executive suite. It's written for high-achievers who are tired of just "managing" their mental health and want to transform it into a source of strength.

The Journey Ahead

The chapters that follow will take you through the complete journey of understanding and overcoming the mental health challenges that plague high-achievers. We'll explore:

- Why successful people are often the most vulnerable to mental health struggles
- How your brain responds to chronic stress and trauma
- The self-sabotaging patterns that keep you stuck
- Why vulnerability is actually a leadership superpower
- How to break free from co-dependent relationships that drain your energy
- Techniques for managing anxious predictions and limiting beliefs
- The art of controlling what you can and releasing what you can't

- Mindfulness practices that work for busy executives
- How to rewire your mind for sustained success and wellbeing

Each chapter includes practical exercises and tools that you can implement immediately. These aren't theoretical concepts—they're battle-tested strategies that helped me rebuild my life and emerge stronger than before.

A Note on Therapy

Initially, I was sceptical about Cognitive Behavioural Therapy (CBT). I'd experienced group sessions before and hadn't gotten much from them. But I was connected with Christine, an exceptional therapist who changed my perspective entirely. Throughout this book, I'll share insights from our work together, including the profound question she asked me in our first session: "Who is John?"

After much thought, my answer was honest and troubling: "I don't know anymore."

Christine told me that by the end of our sessions, I would know myself, my values, and my core beliefs. I would clearly know the answer to that question. She was right, and this book is part of that discovery process—both for me and, I hope, for you.

The Butterfly: A Symbol of Transformation

The butterfly features prominently throughout this book's journey because it represents the profound transformation that's possible when we embrace our struggles rather than simply enduring them. During my therapy with Christine, she spoke about butterflies frequently, and their symbolism became central to understanding my own metamorphosis.

Christine explained that my identity had been all about being the CEO of the business—I was trapped in the cocoon of executive performance, getting little pleasure from it, and it was impacting my health. She helped me understand that, like a caterpillar entering its cocoon, I needed to surrender my old identity to emerge as something entirely new.

The butterfly's journey mirrors our own path through mental health challenges:

- The caterpillar stage represents our old patterns and limitations
- The cocoon represents the difficult period of breakdown and transformation
- The emergence represents our rebirth into greater wisdom and capability
- The flight represents living with new freedom and authentic power

Just as the butterfly's metamorphosis isn't just about getting back to being a caterpillar—it's about becoming something entirely new and more beautiful than could have been imagined—our journey through mental health challenges isn't just about recovery. It's about transformation into who we were always meant to become.

If you're reading this book, chances are you're facing your own version of that moment in Thailand. You might be lying awake at 3

AM with racing thoughts, or feeling overwhelmed despite your external success, or simply sensing that "OK" isn't good enough anymore.

You're not alone. And more importantly, there is a way forward.

Let's begin

Chapter 1

The Human Behind the Executive Mask - Learning from the Butterfly

"The most powerful leadership tool you have is your own personal example."

— John Wooden

In the corporate world, CEOs and senior executives are often viewed as larger-than-life figures—unshakeable, decisive, and always in control. They're expected to drive multi-million-pound enterprises, manage teams with unwavering confidence, and consistently deliver results regardless of market conditions or personal circumstances. But behind every title, and every confident presentation, lies a simple truth that we often forget: leaders are human beings first.

This fundamental reality—that executives are as vulnerable to stress, self-doubt, exhaustion, and emotional turmoil as anyone else—is something our business culture systematically ignores. We've created an environment where admitting struggle is seen as weakness, where seeking help is viewed as incompetence, and where the very qualities that make someone an effective leader become the tools of their own destruction.

Like the butterfly trapped in its cocoon, many leaders find themselves imprisoned by their own success, unable to break free from patterns that once served them but now limit their growth and wellbeing.

The Butterfly's Lesson: Embracing Transformation

Christine spoke about butterflies at many of our sessions, and their symbolism became central to my recovery. I remember very clearly that she asked me, "Who is John?" My answer after much thought was that I didn't know anymore. Christine informed me that by the end of our sessions, I would know myself, my values and core beliefs clearly.

She explained that my identity had become all about being the CEO of the business—I was trapped in the cocoon of executive performance, gaining little real satisfaction from it, while my health suffered greatly. Like a caterpillar that must surrender its familiar form to become something magnificent, I needed to release my old identity to discover who I truly was beneath the professional persona.

As humans, we can learn several important lessons from the butterfly that are particularly relevant for leaders struggling with their mental health and authentic identity:

The Importance of Embracing Change

Just like a butterfly emerges from a cocoon, humans can learn to embrace significant life changes and see them as opportunities for personal growth. Some changes happen that we cannot control, and this can cause us to be unsettled and overthink the situation. If we learn to embrace these changes and see them as exciting opportunities to learn and develop, we can progress and move away from objectless fear.

The butterfly doesn't resist its transformation—it surrenders to the process, trusting that something beautiful will emerge. As leaders, we often resist change because we fear losing control or revealing our vulnerabilities. But like the butterfly, our greatest growth comes through embracing rather than fighting the process of transformation.

The Power of Patience in Transformation

I am exceptionally impatient and want things to happen now. Learning to live with discomfort and uncertainty is very challenging and can use enormous energy. However, it's important to stay patient and take time to accept change and move through the change curve. Being able to self-reflect and see where you are on the change curve can help you be more patient and trust the process.

A saying I have always held onto is "If you follow the process, the results will look after themselves." The butterfly's metamorphosis takes time, teaching us to be patient and trust the process of change. There's no rushing the transformation—attempts to emerge too early only damage the delicate wings that are still forming.

Resilience Through Difficulty: Learning from the Storm

I was fascinated to understand what a butterfly does in a storm. Butterflies are beautiful creatures that are also very delicate. In a storm, as you would expect, the butterfly seeks shelter. What it also does is fold up its wings. If a butterfly's wings become exceptionally wet and damaged, the butterfly can't fly and its life will end.

Once the storm has passed, the butterfly will come out from its place of shelter and resume activity.

When I reflected on these facts and compared them to my own situation, it demonstrated the need to rest and take shelter in the middle of a storm and to also know that the storm will pass, even if it doesn't feel like it will.

The last 12 months of my career were one hell of a storm. What I didn't do was look after myself through the storm. I took all the positive steps once my body and mind had given me no choice but to rest and recuperate.

This goes deeper than making simple decisions. We have all been shaped over our lifetime through our values and beliefs. I was always striving for more and always had to prove my worth to others. Many successful people are driven by fear. There's nothing fundamentally wrong with this; however, it's important to be self-aware. If you're driven by fear, your chances of burnout or mental health challenges increase dramatically. You'll be striving to prove your worth whilst using enormous emotional energy overthinking, analysing, and worrying about what you're fearful of.

My learning from this is to ensure that when we are in challenging times, it's even more important to take positive steps to keep ourselves healthy. Exercise, diet, and sleep have all been crucial in my recovery—the lesson being they are crucial all the time.

Despite their delicate appearance, butterflies are resilient creatures, reminding us to persevere through challenges whilst also knowing when to seek shelter and protection.

Freedom and Joy: The Butterfly's Gift

The butterfly's ability to fly represents freedom and the ability to experience life with lightness and joy. Whilst we can't fly, we can still make sure we live in the present and take joy from the world around us. Being with nature is proven to help improve our mental health. It makes us happier and calmer, and it's proven to help lower blood pressure. Being outside and exposed to natural light will help with sleep as it helps regulate the sleep and wake cycles.

I understand that at times it can be difficult to motivate ourselves when suffering from low mood or constant worry. Even going for a walk can be asking too much when in a depressive episode, so I suggest beginning with a smaller step—simply stand outside and take a moment to observe and listen. Ask yourself: What can I see? What can I hear? This gentle practice helps to shift your attention away from intrusive thoughts and bring your focus back to the present and to the world immediately around you.

Self-Discovery: The Journey from Caterpillar to Butterfly

The transformation from caterpillar to butterfly can be seen as a journey of self-discovery and understanding one's potential. When I look back over my career, I have immense pride and satisfaction. I have gratitude for the leaders I have worked for who trusted me and helped me grow. I also reflect on leadership experiences that challenged me deeply. I've encountered as many leadership styles that didn't align with my values as those that did - and learning from both has been exceptionally powerful.

When I left school at 16, all I wanted to do was work and earn some money. I had little interest in school and found the style of teaching made it more difficult for me to learn and retain information. I have since found a huge joy for learning and thirst for knowledge; however, I have also established that learning through observing, being coached, and going on a journey of self-discovery has the biggest impact in terms of changing behaviour and embedding knowledge and skills.

The leaders I have admired most have all been very competent coaches. They have all shown an interest in me as a person, trusted me, and empowered me through the autonomy they gave me. This has applied to the boss who appointed me as a Bank Manager at the age of 21 and the boss who appointed me as CEO of a regulated sector business. These leaders empowered me, supported me, and gave me the space to discover for myself the most effective ways to run my business.

Learning and discovering about yourself is a lifelong journey. The lessons learnt from success and failure are both powerful. Taking the time to stop and reflect is so important. It enables you to understand your thoughts, emotions, and behaviours better.

Like the butterfly emerging from its cocoon, this process of self-discovery reveals capabilities and beauty we didn't know existed within us. The caterpillar could never imagine flight, just as we often can't imagine the potential that lies within our struggles and challenges.

Acceptance of Discomfort: The Cocoon Stage

The process of metamorphosis can be uncomfortable for the caterpillar, teaching us to embrace discomfort as a necessary part of growth. The cocoon stage—that dark, confined space where everything familiar dissolves—mirrors the difficult periods in our lives when we must release old patterns to make room for new possibilities.

Accepting discomfort means acknowledging and allowing negative emotions rather than trying to suppress them. I found this particularly challenging, as it is deeply uncomfortable to sit with your feelings, especially when they are intense or unsettling. When your mind is flooded with emotional thoughts and your inner dialogue turns into a stream of negativity, acceptance becomes exceedingly difficult.

I was told that I was going through grief for how I wanted things to be and how they used to be. Grief to me was an emotion experienced following the death of a loved one—it wasn't something connected with my job and emotional state. I now know that grief comes to us in many forms and due to many situations and accepting that we need to grieve is powerful.

Just as the caterpillar must surrender its familiar form in the darkness of the cocoon, we must sometimes surrender our familiar identities and patterns to discover who we're truly meant to become. The butterfly emerges not as an improved caterpillar, but as an entirely new creature with capabilities it never possessed before.

The Butterfly Emerges: From Breakdown to Breakthrough

My breakdown in Thailand represented my cocoon stage—that dark, uncomfortable period where everything familiar dissolved. I had been operating as "CEO John" for so long that I had forgotten who existed beneath the professional persona. Like the caterpillar that must completely dissolve in the cocoon before reforming as a butterfly, I had to let go of my old identity to discover my authentic self.

The process was terrifying. In the cocoon, the caterpillar literally dissolves into what biologists call "imaginal soup"—it becomes formless, undefined, uncertain. During my darkest moments of recovery, I felt similarly dissolved. I didn't know who I was without my executive identity, without the constant demands and familiar pressures.

But just as the caterpillar carries within it the imaginal cells that will become the butterfly's wings, I carried within me the seeds of who I was meant to become. The breakdown wasn't the end of my story—it was the necessary dissolution that allowed for authentic transformation.

The Butterfly's Wings: New Capabilities

When the butterfly emerges, it possesses capabilities the caterpillar never had—the ability to fly, to see the world from new perspectives, to access nectar from flowers that were unreachable before. Similarly, my journey through mental health challenges gave me capabilities I never possessed as a purely performance-driven executive:

Authentic Leadership: Instead of leading from a facade of perfection, I learned to lead from genuine humanity and vulnerability

Emotional Intelligence: The depth of my own emotional experience gave me a greater capacity to understand and support others

Resilience: Having navigated a genuine crisis, I developed unshakeable confidence in my ability to handle whatever challenges arise

Perspective: The butterfly sees the garden differently than the caterpillar—my struggles gave me a new perspective on what truly matters in leadership and life

Compassion: Understanding my own struggles created deep empathy for others facing similar challenges

These weren't just improvements to my existing capabilities—they were entirely new ways of being that weren't possible before the transformation.

The Flight: Living with New Freedom

The butterfly doesn't fly to escape its past as a caterpillar—it flies because flight is now its nature. Similarly, the growth that emerged from my mental health journey isn't about running from difficulty but about living from a new centre of authentic strength.

This new way of being includes:

- Making decisions from wisdom rather than fear
- Building relationships based on genuine connection rather than professional utility
- Finding joy and meaning in the process rather than just the outcomes
- Leading others in ways that develop their own wings rather than keeping them dependent
- Accepting challenges as opportunities for continued growth rather than threats to avoid

The butterfly doesn't struggle to fly—it's simply expressing its true nature. After my transformation, authentic leadership doesn't feel like effort—it's simply who I am now.

The Cultural Programming

Think about how leaders are portrayed in business media. They're always "smashing it," "dominating the market," or "revolutionising their industry." When they speak at conferences or give interviews, they present polished success stories with clear trajectories from challenge to triumph. What they don't share are the sleepless nights, the moments of crushing self-doubt, or the times they sat in their car after a difficult board meeting and wondered if they were failing everyone who depended on them.

This cultural conditioning runs deep. From business school case studies to leadership development programmes, we're taught to project strength and certainty even when we feel neither. We learn to speak in confident absolutes, to make decisive decisions even with incomplete information, and to inspire others even when our own motivation is running low.

The Isolation of Leadership

One of the most challenging aspects of senior leadership is the inherent isolation it creates. The higher you climb, the fewer people you can speak to openly about your struggles. Your direct reports look to you for stability and direction. Your board expects confidence and results. Your family often bears the brunt of your stress without fully understanding its source.

During my most difficult period as CEO, I felt completely alone despite being surrounded by people all day. In meetings, I was the one everyone turned to for answers. At home, I was distracted and not completely present.

This isolation isn't just uncomfortable—it's psychologically dangerous. Humans are social creatures who need connection and support to maintain mental health. When leaders cut themselves off from authentic relationships due to their role's demands, they create a perfect storm for anxiety, depression, and burnout.

The Real Cost of Perfectionism

The drive for perfection that often propels people to leadership positions can become their greatest liability. In my case, perfectionism wasn't just about doing good work—it became mentally very challenging as my best work could not deliver the results required due to the circumstances surrounding me.

The Performance Trap

As leaders, we become addicted to performance. We measure our worth by results, our value by outcomes, and our identity by achievements. This creates what I call the "performance trap"—a cycle where our self-esteem becomes entirely dependent on external validation and measurable success.

When I was appointed CEO, my identity became completely wrapped up in the role. I wasn't John, who happened to be a CEO; I was CEO John, and everything else became secondary. My relationships, my hobbies, my personal interests—all of it took a backseat to the demands of performance.

This wouldn't have been sustainable even in the best circumstances, but I was appointed to turn around a business facing significant challenges. The parent company was experiencing considerable instability at senior leadership level, with frequent changes that required me to repeatedly re-establish relationships and credibility.

The pressure was relentless, and because I had tied my entire identity to professional success, every setback felt like an existential threat.

The Feedback Loop of Stress

What many leaders don't realise is that chronic stress creates a feedback loop that impairs the very capabilities they need most. When your nervous system is constantly activated, your decision-making suffers, your creativity diminishes, and your ability to connect with others deteriorates.

I noticed this in myself during the final months before my breakdown. I was working longer hours but accomplishing less. I was having more meetings but making fewer meaningful decisions. I was talking to more people but feeling less connected to my team. The harder I tried to perform, the worse my performance became, which only increased my anxiety and perpetuated the cycle.

The Neuroscience of Leadership Under Stress

Understanding what happens in your brain when you're under chronic stress can be transformative for leaders. It helps explain why the strategies that worked for you in the past might suddenly stop working, and why simply "trying harder" often makes things worse.

The Hijacked Executive Function

Your prefrontal cortex—the part of your brain responsible for executive functions like planning, decision-making, and emotional regulation—is also the most vulnerable to stress. When you're in chronic fight-or-flight mode, blood flow and resources are redirected away from this crucial area towards more primitive survival centres.

This means that during the times when you most need clear thinking and sound judgement, your brain is least equipped to provide them. You might find yourself making impulsive decisions, struggling to see the big picture, or feeling emotionally reactive in situations where you'd normally be calm and measured.

The Memory and Learning Impact

Chronic stress also affects your hippocampus, the brain region responsible for learning and memory formation. This explains why you might feel like you're not learning from experience or why solutions that worked in the past seem to slip from your grasp when you need them most.

During my most stressful period, I felt like I was losing my edge. Strategies that had served me well throughout my career seemed ineffective. I questioned whether I was losing my abilities, when my brain was simply operating in survival mode rather than optimisation mode.

Breaking the Silence: Leaders Who Spoke Truth

One of the most powerful moments in my journey was learning about other high-profile leaders who had publicly acknowledged their mental health struggles. These examples helped me realise that seeking help wasn't a sign of weakness—it was a sign of wisdom.

Antonio Horta-Osorio: A Banking CEO's Courage

When Antonio Horta-Osorio, the CEO of Lloyds Banking Group, took leave for mental health reasons in 2011, it sent shockwaves through the financial world. Here was the leader of Britain's biggest retail bank, openly acknowledging that he needed help.

In his own words: "I was very mindful that the bank was in a very weak position to face adversity. It was a problem that was going around my mind constantly, which led me to sleep less and less. And the less and less sleep progressively led me to exhaustion, and then to not sleeping at all, which was a form of torture, so I had to address it and I did."

What struck me most about his story wasn't just that he took time off—it was what he did when he returned. He implemented comprehensive mental health programmes throughout the organisation, trained thousands of mental health first aiders, and elevated the conversation about psychological wellbeing in the workplace.

His personal experience led him to understand a crucial truth: "At least one out of three people goes through a mental health problem throughout their lifetime. So, it is actually much more common than you might think."

Arianna Huffington: Redefining Success

Arianna Huffington's wake-up call came in 2007 when she collapsed from exhaustion due to chronic overwork, breaking her cheekbone in the fall. This moment led her to completely rethink her approach to leadership and success.

Rather than viewing this breakdown as a failure, she reframed it as a necessary course correction. She later founded Thrive Global, a company dedicated to addressing workplace burnout and promoting well-being. Her story demonstrates how leaders can transform their personal struggles into systematic solutions that benefit others.

The Power of Vulnerable Leadership

Contrary to popular belief, vulnerability in leadership isn't weakness—it's a superpower. When leaders are willing to acknowledge their humanity, it creates psychological safety that allows entire organisations to perform at higher levels.

Building Trust Through Authenticity

When I finally began to open up about my struggles, something remarkable happened. Instead of losing respect from my team, I gained it. Rather than losing my team's respect, I earned more of it. Instead of seeming weak, I appeared more human—and, as a result, more trustworthy. Team members started to share their own challenges and concerns, enabling us to address issues earlier and far more effectively.

One conversation stands out particularly clearly. I was speaking with a junior team member who was quite experienced in terms of length of service and knowledge of her role—a real asset to the business. I called her by her first name when chatting informally and she went bright red but had a beaming smile. I asked her why she was smiling, and her response was, "You've used my name." I asked her to explain as I was a bit confused. She explained to me that no one in a senior position before had just chatted to her and used her name. Such a simple thing for me to do that seemed to make a big difference to her.

Creating Psychological Safety

Google's extensive research on high-performing teams identified psychological safety as the number one factor in team effectiveness. Psychological safety exists when team members feel safe to be vulnerable, to admit mistakes, to ask questions, and to propose new ideas without fear of negative consequences.

Leaders create psychological safety not by being perfect, but by modelling the behaviour they want to see. When you acknowledge your own uncertainties, admit your mistakes, and show that you're still learning, you give others permission to do the same.

Practical Strategies for Human-Centred Leadership

Recognising that your human is just the first step. The real work lies in developing practices that honour your humanity whilst still meeting the demands of leadership.

The Daily Check-In

One of the simplest yet most powerful practices I developed was a daily emotional check-in. Before jumping into emails or meetings, I would spend five minutes asking myself:

- How am I feeling right now?
- What do I need today to be effective?

- What signs of stress should I watch for?
- How can I take care of myself whilst taking care of others?

This practice helped me recognise early warning signs of overwhelm and take proactive steps to address them before they became crises.

The Support Network Audit

Take an honest look at your support network. Who are the people in your life who see you as a person first and a leader second? Who can you talk to without worrying about their expectations or judgements?

For many leaders, this audit reveals a concerning truth: their support network has shrunk as their responsibilities have grown. If this is the case for you, it's time to intentionally rebuild these relationships.

Consider:
- Joining a CEO peer group or executive coaching programme
- Maintaining friendships outside your industry
- Working with a therapist who understands executive stress
- Developing relationships with mentors who've navigated similar challenges

The Boundary Setting Practice

Leaders often struggle with boundaries because their role seems to demand constant availability. However, sustainable leadership requires protecting your mental and physical resources.

Start by identifying your non-negotiables:

- What time do you stop checking emails?
- What days or hours are protected for personal time?
- What types of requests do you automatically delegate?
- How do you maintain perspective during crisis situations?

The Role of Cognitive Behavioural Therapy for Leaders

When I finally began working with Christine, my CBT therapist, I was sceptical. Therapy felt like an admission of failure, and CBT seemed too structured for someone who prided himself on creative problem-solving. I was wrong on both counts.

CBT for Executive Decision-Making

CBT techniques are particularly powerful for leaders because they address the cognitive distortions that can derail executive judgement:

Catastrophic Thinking: When you immediately jump to worst-case scenarios.

All-or-Nothing Thinking: When you see only success or failure with no middle ground.

Mind Reading: When you assume you know what others are thinking.

Fortune Telling: When you predict negative outcomes without evidence.

These distortions are especially dangerous for leaders because they influence not just personal well-being but organisational decision-making.

The Thought Record Technique

One of the most valuable tools Christine taught me was the thought record—a systematic way of examining and challenging problematic thoughts. Here's how it works:

1. Situation: What triggered the difficult emotion?

2. Emotion: What are you feeling and how intensely (1-10)?

3. Automatic Thought: What went through your mind?

4. Evidence For: What supports this thought?

5. Evidence Against: What contradicts this thought?

6. Balanced Thought: What's a more realistic perspective?

7. New Emotion: How do you feel now (1-10)?

For example, my thought record might look like:

Situation: Difficult questions from executive member

Emotion: Anxiety (8/10)

Automatic Thought: "They're losing confidence in me."

Evidence For: They asked challenging questions.

Evidence Against: Challenging questions are their job; they've supported me through difficult times before.

Balanced Thought: "They're doing their due diligence; this is normal governance."

New Emotion: Concern (4/10)

This process doesn't eliminate difficult emotions, but it prevents them from spiralling into panic or despair.

Questions for Self-Reflection

As you reflect on your own leadership journey, consider these questions:

1. What beliefs do I hold about leadership that might be contributing to my stress?
2. How often do I prioritise self-care, and what prevents me from doing so more frequently?
3. Have I ever experienced burnout, and how did it affect my decision-making and relationships?
4. How do I currently manage negative thoughts or self-doubt? Could I improve my approach?
5. What small changes can I implement today to improve my well-being without compromising my effectiveness?
6. Who can I turn to for support when I feel overwhelmed, and how often do I reach out?
7. What would I tell a struggling colleague that I'm not telling myself?
8. How can I create a culture that encourages self-care and work-life integration for my team?

The Butterfly's Wisdom for Modern Leaders

We will return to the butterfly's wisdom as we explore the practical tools and strategies for transformation. Just as the butterfly's metamorphosis follows natural stages, so does our journey toward authentic leadership and mental well-being.

The butterfly teaches us that:

- **Breakdown can be a breakthrough**: What appears to be destruction is often reconstruction
- **Patience with process**: Transformation cannot be forced or rushed
- **Trust in emergence**: Even when we can't see the outcome, the process is working
- **New capabilities await**: We will emerge with abilities we never knew we possessed
- **Flight is possible**: Freedom and joy are not just dreams but our natural state when we live authentically

As we explore the neuroscience of trauma, the patterns of self-sabotage, the courage of vulnerability, and the practices of mindful leadership, remember the butterfly's promise: you are not just recovering from breakdown—you are transforming into something magnificent.

Your cocoon stage—whether it's happening now or has already passed—is not your end but your beginning. The leader emerging from this process will possess depth, wisdom, and authentic power that your previous self could never have imagined.

The butterfly doesn't mourn its caterpillar days or try to crawl back into its cocoon. It spreads its wings and flies, knowing that flight was always its destiny—it just had to go through the darkness to discover the light.

Moving Forward

The journey towards sustainable leadership begins with a simple acknowledgement: you are human first, leader second. This isn't a weakness to overcome—it's a strength to embrace.

In the chapters that follow, we'll explore the specific tools and strategies that can help you honour your humanity whilst excelling in your role. We'll dive deep into understanding how your brain responds to stress, how to identify and interrupt self-sabotaging patterns, and how to build the mental resilience that allows for both high performance and personal wellbeing.

Remember: seeking help isn't an admission of failure—it's a commitment to being the leader your team, your organisation, and your family truly need.

You are not just a CEO, an executive, or a leader. You are a human being first. And that humanity, when properly understood and cared for, becomes your greatest leadership asset.

Chapter 2
When Your Brain Betrays You - Understanding Trauma and Fear

"The body keeps the score. It remembers everything."

— Bessel van der Kolk

When Christine first used the word "trauma" in our therapy sessions, I physically recoiled. Trauma, in my understanding, was reserved for people who had experienced the most severe circumstances—natural disasters, violent crimes, combat, or serious accidents. I was a CEO dealing with work stress. Surely that didn't qualify as trauma.

This resistance to the word "trauma" is common amongst high achievers. We minimise our experiences, comparing our stress to "real" trauma and finding ourselves lacking in legitimacy. But this perspective misses a crucial truth: trauma isn't just about what happens to you—it's about how your nervous system responds to prolonged threat and stress.

What I learnt through my journey changed everything about how I understood my breakdown and, more importantly, how I could heal from it.

Redefining Trauma for High-Achievers

Traditional definitions of trauma focus on single, severe events. But there's another type of trauma that's particularly relevant for leaders and high performers: complex trauma, also known as chronic stress trauma. This occurs when someone is exposed to ongoing stressful situations over extended periods, especially when those situations feel inescapable.

Workplace Trauma: A Hidden Epidemic

Consider my situation: three years of working to transform a challenged business whilst the parent company experienced significant leadership transitions. Each change meant starting over - re-establishing credibility, re-explaining strategy, and adapting to new priorities.

This type of workplace trauma is far more common than we acknowledge, especially in senior leadership roles where:

- The stakes are consistently high
- Personal identity becomes fused with professional performance
- Support systems are limited due to confidentiality and isolation
- The pressure to appear strong prevents help-seeking behaviour
- Decision-making affects many people's livelihoods

The Neurobiology of Chronic Stress

Your brain doesn't distinguish between a physical threat and a psychological one. When you're in chronic fight-or-flight mode—which many executives are for months or years at a time—your nervous system undergoes the same changes as someone who's experienced acute trauma.

The Amygdala: Your Internal Alarm System

The amygdala, your brain's threat-detection centre, becomes hyperactive under chronic stress. It starts seeing danger everywhere, even in routine situations. For me, this meant that normal business challenges—difficult conversations, board presentations, or strategic decisions—began triggering the same physiological response as genuine emergencies.

I noticed this escalation in myself during my final months as CEO. Situations I had once handled with calm confidence began to feel overwhelming. My heart would race during ordinary meetings, and I found myself catastrophising over minor setbacks. My sleep became fragmented, as my mind refused to switch off from its constant state of threat scanning.

The Hippocampus: Memory and Learning

Chronic stress literally shrinks your hippocampus, the brain region responsible for memory formation and contextual learning. This explains why, during my most stressful period, I felt like I was losing my edge. Strategies that had worked throughout my career seemed to slip away when I needed them most.

More troubling, I began having difficulty learning from positive experiences. Even when things went well, my brain couldn't seem to encode these successes in a way that built confidence for future challenges. Every day felt like starting from scratch.

The Prefrontal Cortex: Executive Function Under Siege

Perhaps most relevant for leaders, chronic stress impairs the prefrontal cortex—the brain region responsible for executive functions like strategic thinking, emotional regulation, and sound judgement. When this area is compromised, you might experience:

- Difficulty seeing the big picture
- Impulsive decision-making
- Emotional reactivity in situations where you'd normally be measured
- Trouble prioritising effectively
- Decreased creative problem-solving ability

During my breakdown period, I noticed all these symptoms. I was working harder than ever but felt less effective. I was spending more time on decisions but feeling less confident in them. I was having more meetings but accomplishing less meaningful work.

The Trauma Response: Fight, Flight, Freeze, and Fawn

Understanding your body's trauma responses can help you recognise when you're operating from a place of stress rather than choice. Whilst most people know about fight-or-flight, there are four primary trauma responses, each with distinct implications for leaders.

Fight: The Aggressive Response

The fight response manifests as anger, aggression, or confrontational behaviour. In leadership contexts, this might look like:

- Becoming unusually critical or demanding with your team
- Feeling irritated by normal workplace interactions
- Having a shorter fuse in meetings or negotiations
- Micromanaging due to anxiety about outcomes

Flight: The Avoidance Response

Flight responses involve avoiding or escaping stressful situations. For executives, this often appears as:

- Procrastinating on difficult decisions
- Delegating everything to avoid responsibility
- Working from home to avoid face-to-face interactions
- Mentally "checking out" during challenging conversations

Freeze: The Shutdown Response

The freeze response involves becoming immobilised when faced with stress. In leadership roles, this can manifest as:

- Analysis paralysis when facing decisions
- Feeling mentally blank during important presentations
- Being unable to respond effectively to crisis situations
- Physical sensations of heaviness or numbness

Fawn: The People-Pleasing Response

The fawn response involves appeasing others to avoid conflict or abandonment. For leaders, this often appears as:

- Saying yes to every request to avoid disappointing people
- Over-accommodating difficult personalities

- Avoiding necessary but uncomfortable decisions
- Prioritising others' comfort over organisational needs

The Physiology of Fear: What Happens in Your Body

Trauma and chronic stress don't just affect your mind—they create profound changes in your body that can persist long after the stressful situation has ended.

The Nervous System: Stuck in High Alert

Your autonomic nervous system has two primary branches:

- **Sympathetic**: The "accelerator" that activates fight-or-flight responses.
- **Parasympathetic**: The "brake" that promotes rest, digestion, and recovery.

Under chronic stress, your sympathetic nervous system becomes chronically activated, whilst your parasympathetic system becomes suppressed. This creates a state where your body is constantly prepared for emergency action, even when none is needed.

Physical symptoms I experienced included:

- Rapid heart rate, even at rest.
- Shallow breathing or feeling like I couldn't get enough air.
- Muscle tension, particularly in my shoulders and back.
- Digestive issues and changes in appetite.
- Sleep disruption and chronic fatigue.
- Feeling "wired but tired"—simultaneously exhausted and unable to relax.

The Stress Hormone Cascade

Chronic activation of your stress response system leads to persistently elevated levels of stress hormones like cortisol and adrenaline. Whilst these hormones are helpful in short bursts, chronic elevation creates serious health consequences:

Cortisol Effects:

- Impaired immune function
- Increased blood pressure
- Disrupted sleep patterns
- Mood instability
- Weight gain, particularly around the midsection
- Decreased bone density

Adrenaline Effects:

- Heart palpitations
- Anxiety and restlessness
- Difficulty concentrating
- Trembling or shakiness
- Increased blood pressure

Breaking the Cycle: Neuroplasticity and Healing

The good news about understanding trauma's impact on your brain is that it also reveals the path to healing. Your brain's neuroplasticity—its ability to form new neural connections throughout your life—means that the changes caused by chronic stress can be reversed.

The Healing Process: Rewiring Your Brain

Healing from trauma isn't about forgetting or "getting over it"—it's about teaching your nervous system that it's safe to relax. This requires both understanding and practice.

Step 1: Recognition and Awareness

The first step is learning to recognise when you're in a trauma response state. This might involve:

- Noticing physical sensations like increased heart rate or muscle tension
- Recognising thought patterns like catastrophising or black-and-white thinking
- Identifying behavioural changes like increased irritability or withdrawal

Step 2: Nervous System Regulation

Once you can recognise activation, you can begin practising regulation techniques:

The Physiological Sigh: A powerful technique for immediate nervous system calming

- Take a normal inhale through your nose
- Take a second, smaller inhale on top of the first
- Exhale slowly through your mouth
- Repeat 2-3 times

This technique works because the double inhale maximally inflates your lungs, triggering a parasympathetic response that calms your nervous system within seconds.

Progressive Muscle Relaxation: Systematically tense and release muscle groups
- Start with your toes and work upward
- Tense each muscle group for 5 seconds, then release
- Notice the contrast between tension and relaxation
- This teaches your body how to physically let go of stress

Step 3: Cognitive Restructuring

Trauma often creates distorted thinking patterns that maintain stress even when the original stressor is gone. Common cognitive distortions include:

- **Catastrophising**: Automatically assuming the worst possible outcome
- **All-or-Nothing Thinking**: Seeing situations as completely successful or complete failures
- **Mind Reading**: Assuming you know what others are thinking (usually negative)
- **Fortune Telling**: Predicting negative outcomes without evidence

Exercise: The ABCDE Model

When you notice distorted thinking, use this framework:

A - Activating Event: What happened?

B - Beliefs: What thoughts went through your mind?

C - Consequences: How did you feel and behave?

D - Dispute: What evidence challenges these thoughts?

E - Energise: How do you feel with more balanced thoughts? For example:

A: Executive member asks challenging questions about strategy

B: "They're losing confidence in me."

C: Anxiety (8/10), defensive responses.

D: They're paid to ask tough questions; they've supported me through challenges before.

E: Concern (4/10), more collaborative responses.

Practical Trauma Recovery Tools for Executives

Recovery from workplace trauma requires tools that fit into demanding schedules whilst providing genuine relief.

The Daily Reset Protocol

Morning Preparation (5 minutes):

- Three deep physiological sighs upon waking
- Set intention for the day: "I am safe, capable, and learning"
- Brief body scan to identify areas of tension

Midday Recalibration (3 minutes):

- Step outside if possible
- Five conscious breaths, focusing on exhale length
- Ask: "What does my body need right now?"

Evening Integration (10 minutes):

- Journal three things that went well, however small
- Progressive muscle relaxation or gentle stretching
- Gratitude practice focusing on support received

The STOP Technique for Acute Stress

When you notice trauma activation during your day:

S - Stop: Pause whatever you're doing

T - Take a breath: One deep, slow breath

O - Observe: What's happening in your body and mind?

P - Proceed: Choose your response rather than reacting automatically

Building Your Resilience Account

Think of resilience as a bank account that you can either drain or replenish through your daily choices:

Deposits (Add to resilience):
- Regular sleep (7-9 hours)
- Nutritious meals at consistent times
- Movement or exercise
- Connection with supportive people
- Engaging in activities you enjoy
- Spending time in nature
- Mindfulness or meditation practice

Withdrawals (Drain resilience):
- Sleep deprivation
- Skipping meals or poor nutrition
- Isolation from supportive relationships
- Overwork without breaks
- Excessive caffeine or alcohol

- Negative self-talk
- Avoiding problems rather than addressing them

Trauma-Informed Leadership

Understanding trauma doesn't just help with personal healing—it makes you a more effective leader. When you recognise trauma responses in yourself and others, you can create environments that promote safety and high performance.

Creating Psychological Safety

Teams perform best when members feel psychologically safe—able to be vulnerable, admit mistakes, and take reasonable risks without fear of punishment or humiliation. Leaders who understand trauma responses can:

- Recognise when team members are in fight, flight, freeze, or fawn responses
- Adjust communication style to promote safety
- Address systemic stressors that might be traumatising staff
- Model healthy responses to setbacks and challenges

The Trauma-Informed Meeting

Consider how standard business practices might inadvertently trigger trauma responses:

- Public criticism or callouts
- Surprise agenda items or ambush conversations
- All-or-nothing deadline pressures
- Unclear expectations or constantly changing priorities

Trauma-informed alternatives might include:

- Private feedback conversations followed by public recognition
- Advance notice of agenda items and meeting purposes
- Realistic timeline discussions that account for unexpected challenges
- Clear, consistent communication about expectations and changes

Moving Forward: Integration and Growth

Healing from trauma isn't about returning to who you were before—it's about integrating your experiences in a way that makes you stronger and more resilient. This process, called post-traumatic growth, can lead to:

- Greater appreciation for life and relationships
- Increased sense of personal strength and capability
- Deeper spiritual or philosophical understanding
- Enhanced empathy and connection with others
- Recognition of new possibilities and opportunities

My own breakdown, whilst incredibly difficult, ultimately led to profound personal and professional growth. I developed a deeper understanding of leadership, stronger relationships with family and colleagues, and tools for managing stress that serve me daily.

The brain that betrayed me under chronic stress became, through healing and understanding, a more resilient and capable instrument than it had ever been before.

Chapter Summary: Key Takeaways

1. **Workplace trauma is real**: Chronic stress in high-pressure roles can create genuine trauma responses that affect brain function and decision-making.

2. **Your nervous system doesn't distinguish between physical and psychological threats**: Extended periods of workplace stress trigger the same neurobiological changes as acute trauma.

3. **Trauma responses (fight, flight, freeze, fawn) are automatic**: Recognition allows you to choose conscious responses rather than unconscious reactions.

4. **Neuroplasticity enables healing**: Your brain's ability to form new connections means trauma's effects can be reversed with proper techniques and practice.

5. **Recovery requires both understanding and action**: Knowledge alone isn't enough; healing requires consistent practice of regulation techniques.

6. **Trauma-informed leadership is more effective**: Understanding these concepts makes you a better leader by helping you create psychologically safe environments.

In our next chapter, we'll explore how trauma and chronic stress contribute to self-sabotaging behaviours—the unconscious patterns that keep us stuck even when we desperately want to change.

Chapter 3
The Self-Sabotage Trap –
How We Become Our Own Worst Enemy

"Our deepest fear is not that we are inadequate. Our deepest fear is that we are powerful beyond measure."

— Marianne Williamson

During my therapy with Christine, she made an observation that stopped me cold: "John, you've spent more energy in the last few months fighting yourself than fighting your actual business challenges."

I wanted to argue with her, but I couldn't. As I reflected on my behaviour during those final months as CEO, I realised she was right. I had been downplaying my achievements, creating unnecessary complexity in simple situations, and somehow finding ways to make every success feel temporary or undeserved.

I was sabotaging myself, and I didn't even realise I was doing it.

Self-sabotage is one of the most insidious challenges facing high achievers. It's the voice that whispers "you're not ready yet" when opportunity knocks. It's the pattern of creating problems when things are going too well. It's the tendency to snatch defeat from the jaws of victory, often right when success is within reach.

For executives and leaders, self-sabotage is especially perilous, as it undermines not only their own success but also the wellbeing of entire organisations. When leaders sabotage themselves, they consequently undermine their teams, their companies, and all those who rely on their decisions.

Understanding Self-Sabotage: The Psychology Behind the Behaviour

Self-sabotage isn't a character flaw or a sign of weakness—it's a protective mechanism gone wrong. At its core, self-sabotage represents your subconscious mind's attempt to keep you safe from perceived threats, even when those threats are no longer real or relevant.

The Safety of the Known

Humans are wired to prefer predictable discomfort over unpredictable success. This preference, which served our ancestors well in dangerous environments, can become a liability in modern leadership roles where growth and change are essential for survival.

Consider my situation: I had spent years building competence and confidence in increasingly senior roles. Each promotion brought new challenges, but they were challenges I could eventually master. Becoming CEO of a business facing complex challenges, however, represented a level of uncertainty and responsibility that my subconscious mind perceived as dangerous.

Rather than consciously acknowledging my fear, I began unconsciously creating familiar problems. My subconscious was trying to return me to the familiar territory of "struggling but competent" rather than allowing me to succeed in unfamiliar ways.

The Imposter Syndrome Connection

Self-sabotage and imposter syndrome are closely linked. Imposter syndrome is the persistent feeling that you're a fraud who will eventually be exposed, despite evidence of your competence and achievements. For many high-achievers, success feels like a case of mistaken identity rather than earned recognition.

When I became CEO, part of me believed I had somehow fooled everyone into thinking I was qualified for the role. This belief created a constant anxiety that I would be "found out." Self-sabotage became a way of controlling the narrative—if I failed, it would be because of my actions, not because I was fundamentally inadequate.

This dynamic is particularly strong amongst leaders who have experienced rapid career progression. Success can feel unearned or unstable, leading to behaviours designed to prove the impostor syndrome voice right rather than risk having it proven wrong by someone else.

The Many Faces of Executive Self-Sabotage

Self-sabotage in leadership roles takes unique forms that can be difficult to recognise because they often look like dedication, perfectionism, or strategic thinking.

Perfectionism: The Disguised Saboteur

Perfectionism appears virtuous—who wouldn't want a leader who strives for excellence? But perfectionism often becomes a sophisticated form of procrastination and self-sabotage.

The insidious nature of perfectionist self-sabotage is that it feels productive. You're working hard, paying attention to details, and striving for quality. But underneath, you're using perfection as a reason to avoid the vulnerability that comes with putting your work into the world, where it can be evaluated and potentially criticised.

The Success Ceiling

Many high-achievers have an unconscious "success ceiling"—a level of achievement beyond which they don't feel safe or deserving. This ceiling is often set by childhood experiences, family messaging, or cultural conditioning.

For me, becoming CEO represented breaking through a ceiling I didn't even know existed. When I achieved something beyond my unconscious limit, my self-sabotage would kick in to bring me back to familiar territory. I would:

- Downplay achievements in conversations with others
- Focus obsessively on problems rather than celebrating successes
- Create new challenges to maintain a sense of struggle
- Attribute successes to luck rather than skill or effort

The Control Paradox

Executives are typically control-oriented people—it's often part of what makes them effective leaders. However, this need for control can become self-sabotaging when it leads to micromanagement, inability to delegate, or resistance to necessary changes.

This behaviour creates exactly the opposite of what is wanted: instead of increasing control, it decreases effectiveness and creates more problems to manage.

The Neuroscience of Self-Sabotage

Understanding what happens in your brain during self-sabotage can help you recognise and interrupt these patterns before they derail your progress.

The Amygdala's False Alarms

Your amygdala, 'the emotional brain,' is the brain's alarm system, and it doesn't distinguish between physical and psychological threats. When you're approaching a new level of success or responsibility, you may interpret this unfamiliarity as danger and trigger protective responses.

These responses can include:

- **Increased anxiety** around positive opportunities
- **Hypervigilance** for potential problems or threats
- **Risk aversion** even when risks are manageable
- **Catastrophic thinking** about potential negative outcomes

I noticed this pattern before important presentations or meetings. Even when I was well-prepared, my nervous system would activate as if I were facing genuine danger. This activation would then trigger physical body sensations such as headaches, increased heart rate and a feeling of exhaustion afterwards.

The Reticular Activating System (RAS)

Your RAS is a network of neurons in your brain stem that acts as a filter, determining what information gets your conscious attention. It's why you suddenly notice a particular car model everywhere after you decide to buy one.

When you have unconscious beliefs about your limitations or unworthiness, your RAS filters information to support these beliefs. You'll notice your mistakes more than your successes, remember criticism more vividly than praise, and focus on problems rather than opportunities.

Changing self-sabotage patterns requires consciously training your RAS to notice evidence that contradicts limiting beliefs. This is why keeping a success journal or actively acknowledging achievements is so important—you're literally rewiring your brain to notice positive data.

Identifying Your Self-Sabotage Patterns

Self-sabotage is highly individual. What trips up one person might not affect another at all. The key is developing awareness of your specific patterns so you can recognise them in real-time.

Common Self-Sabotage Triggers for Leaders

Success Triggers: Ironically, success itself often triggers self-sabotage. When things are going well, you might unconsciously create problems to return to familiar struggle.

Visibility Triggers: Opportunities for recognition or increased responsibility can trigger fears of exposure and inadequacy.

Decision Triggers: High-stakes decisions can activate perfectionism and analysis paralysis.

Relationship Triggers: Situations requiring vulnerability or trust can trigger protective behaviours that damage connections.

The Self-Sabotage Audit

Take time to honestly assess your patterns across different areas:

Professional Self-Sabotage:

- Do I procrastinate on important but non-urgent tasks?
- Do I downplay my achievements when talking to others?
- Do I create unnecessary complexity in straightforward situations?
- Do I avoid delegation due to fear of others' mistakes?
- Do I seek perfection as a way to avoid judgement?

Personal Self-Sabotage:

- Do I push people away when relationships become too intimate?
- Do I make lifestyle choices that undermine my professional performance?
- Do I avoid opportunities that could lead to growth or recognition?
- Do I engage in negative self-talk that reinforces limiting beliefs?

Decision-Making Self-Sabotage:

- Do I request more information when I already have enough to decide?
- Do I second-guess decisions that are working well?
- Do I create contingency plans that become excuses not to act?
- Do I avoid making decisions by delegating them unnecessarily?

Breaking Free: Strategies for Overcoming Self-Sabotage

Overcoming self-sabotage requires both awareness and action. You need to recognise the patterns and develop alternative responses that serve your growth rather than your fears.

The Pause Practice

When you notice self-sabotaging thoughts or impulses, practice the pause:

1. **STOP**: Physically pause whatever you're doing
2. **BREATHE**: Take three deep breaths to engage your parasympathetic nervous system
3. **NOTICE**: What am I thinking? What am I feeling? How am I behaving? What am I about to do?
4. **CHOOSE**: What response would serve my growth rather than my fear?

This practice creates space between trigger and response, allowing you to choose conscious action rather than unconscious reaction.

Reframing Your Inner Critic

The voice of self-sabotage often sounds like an inner critic focused on protection rather than growth. Learning to reframe this voice is crucial for sustainable change.

Instead of: "I'm not qualified for this opportunity" **Try**: "I'm growing into this opportunity and learning as I go"

Instead of: "I always mess up important presentations" **Try**: "I'm improving my presentation skills with each opportunity"

Instead of: "I don't deserve this success" **Try**: "I've worked hard and am ready to receive good outcomes"

The goal isn't to eliminate self-doubt but to change your relationship with it. Doubt can provide valuable information about areas where you need support or preparation, but it shouldn't be the primary voice making your decisions.

The Success Integration Process

Many people struggle with self-sabotage because they haven't learnt to properly integrate their successes. Each achievement becomes isolated rather than building towards a cohesive sense of competence and worth.

Daily Success Acknowledgement: Each evening, write down three things you did well that day, however small. Include:

- What you did

- Why was it meaningful
- How does it reflect your character or abilities?

Monthly Achievement Review: Once per month, review your success journal and look for patterns:
- What types of achievements do I consistently ignore or minimise?
- What strengths appear repeatedly in my successes?
- How have I grown since last month?

Annual Identity Update: Once per year, consciously update your self-concept based on evidence from your achievements:
- How has my competence expanded?
- What new challenges am I now capable of handling?
- How can I adjust my self-talk to reflect my current reality?

The Role of Cognitive Behavioural Therapy in Overcoming Self-Sabotage

CBT is particularly effective for self-sabotage because it addresses the thought patterns that drive self-defeating behaviours.

Identifying Cognitive Distortions

Self-sabotage is often driven by distorted thinking patterns. Common distortions that fuel self-sabotage include:

All-or-Nothing Thinking: "If it's not perfect, it's worthless"

Mental Filter: Focusing exclusively on negatives whilst ignoring positives

Disqualifying the Positive: Explaining away achievements as luck or timing

Mind Reading: Assuming others are thinking negatively about you

Fortune Telling: Predicting failure without evidence

Catastrophising: Imagining worst-case scenarios as inevitable

The Thought Challenge Process

When you notice a self-sabotaging thought, challenge it systematically:

1. **What's the thought?** Write it down exactly as it appears in your mind
2. **What's the evidence for this thought?** List concrete facts that support it
3. **What's the evidence against this thought?** List facts that contradict it
4. **What would I tell a friend having this thought?** Often, we're kinder to others than ourselves
5. **What's a more balanced perspective?** Create a realistic thought that acknowledges both challenges and capabilities

Behavioural Experiments

CBT emphasises testing your beliefs through action. If you believe you'll fail at something, the most effective way to challenge this belief is to try it and gather real data about the outcome.

Start with small experiments that test your self-limiting beliefs:

- If you believe you're bad at public speaking, volunteer to give a brief update at a team meeting
- If you think you can't handle criticism, ask for specific feedback on a project
- If you feel unworthy of recognition, nominate yourself for an appropriate award or opportunity

Advanced Self-Sabotage Recovery: Working with Your Unconscious

Surface-level self-sabotage can often be addressed through awareness and conscious effort. But deep-seated patterns may require working with unconscious beliefs and childhood programming.

The Inner Child and Executive Performance

Many self-sabotage patterns originate in childhood experiences and beliefs formed before you had the cognitive capacity to evaluate them critically. The "inner child" carries these early experiences and can influence adult behaviour in unconscious ways.

Common childhood origins of executive self-sabotage:

"Don't get too big for your boots": Messages about staying humble can become unconscious success ceilings

"We don't have the money": Early scarcity experiences can create guilt about earning well or spending on yourself

"Children should be seen and not heard": Can lead to discomfort with visibility and recognition

"You have to work hard for everything": This can make success feel wrong if it comes easily

Healing Your Relationship with Success

Developing a healthy relationship with success often requires healing your relationship with your younger self, who learnt that achievement was dangerous, undeserved, or temporary.

Inner Child Dialogue Exercise:

1. Identify a self-sabotage pattern that's particularly strong
2. Ask yourself: When did I first learn this belief?
3. Imagine speaking to your younger self who learnt this belief
4. What would you want that child to know about success, achievement, and worth?
5. How can you parent yourself differently now?

This process helps you separate childhood survival strategies from adult leadership requirements.

My Personal Journey Through Self-Sabotage

Looking back, I can now see clearly how self-sabotage contributed to my crisis. The patterns were subtle but pervasive.

Recovery required not just recognising these patterns but understanding their protective function. My perfectionism was trying to keep me safe from criticism. My focus on problems was trying to prevent blindside challenges. I was trying to maintain control in an uncontrollable situation.

The breakthrough came when I learnt to appreciate these protective parts of myself whilst choosing different strategies.

Instead of eliminating my inner perfectionist, I gave it a new job: ensuring that I was prepared for important presentations rather than preventing me from taking action. Instead of ignoring my problem-focused tendency, I scheduled specific times for risk assessment rather than letting it dominate my thinking all day.

Creating Self-Sabotage-Resistant Systems

Individual awareness is crucial, but lasting change often requires environmental and systematic support.

Decision-Making Systems

Create decision-making processes that make self-sabotage more difficult:

- Set deadlines for decisions and stick to them
- Define "good enough" criteria in advance
- Use time-boxing for analysis and preparation
- Build in accountability partners who can recognise your patterns

Success Celebration Systems

Most self-saboteurs are terrible at celebrating achievements. Build celebration into your systems:

- Schedule time to acknowledge completed projects
- Share successes with mentors or peer groups
- Create rituals that mark achievement milestones
- Take meaningful breaks between major efforts

Feedback and Support Systems

Self-sabotage thrives in isolation. Build systems that provide an external perspective:

- Regular coaching or therapy sessions
- Peer mentoring groups with other executives
- 360-degree feedback processes that highlight strengths
- Trusted advisors who can recognise when you're sabotaging yourself

Moving Forward: From Self-Sabotage to Self-Support

The goal isn't to eliminate all self-doubt or protective instincts—these can provide valuable information about risks and areas for growth. The goal is to change your relationship with these internal voices, so they inform rather than control your decisions.

Self-support looks like:

- Taking calculated risks rather than avoiding all uncertainty
- Celebrating achievements rather than immediately seeking the next challenge
- Learning from failures without making them mean you're inadequate
- Seeking help and support rather than trying to handle everything alone
- Trusting your capabilities whilst remaining open to growth

Your self-sabotage patterns developed over years or decades—be patient with yourself as you work to change them. Each time you recognise a pattern and choose a different response, you're rewiring your brain and building new neural pathways that support your success rather than undermining it.

In our next chapter, we'll explore one of the most powerful antidotes to self-sabotage: the courage to be vulnerable and the strength that comes from authentic leadership.

Chapter 4

The Courage to Be Vulnerable –

From Weakness to Strength

"Vulnerability is not winning or losing; it's having the courage to show up and be seen when we have no control over the outcome."

— Brené Brown

Three months into my recovery, I found myself sitting in a coffee shop with a former colleague who had reached out after hearing through the grapevine that I was "taking some time off." I had prepared my usual deflection—a vague reference to needing a break and wanting to explore new opportunities. But when he looked me in the eye and asked, "John, are you alright? You look like you've been through hell," something inside me cracked open.

Instead of my rehearsed response, the truth tumbled out. I told him about the breakdown, the panic attacks, the feeling that I was losing my mind. I expected to see judgement, disappointment, or the awkward discomfort that often follows such revelations. Instead, I saw relief.

"Thank God," he said. "I thought I was the only one."

That conversation changed everything for me. It was the moment I began to understand that vulnerability might actually be my greatest strength as a leader.

Redefining Vulnerability in a Leadership Context

For most of my career, I had seen leaders behaving like they should have all the answers. They projected unwavering confidence and never let others see them sweat. This belief system, deeply embedded in traditional business culture, equates vulnerability with weakness and authenticity with incompetence.

But this paradigm is not only wrong—it's dangerous. It creates leaders who are disconnected from their teams, isolated in their struggles, and unable to build the trust necessary for high performance. Worse, it creates organisations where psychological safety is absent, innovation is stifled, and burnout is rampant.

What Vulnerability Actually Means

Vulnerability, as defined by research professor Brené Brown, is "uncertainty, risk, and emotional exposure." In a leadership context, this translates to:

- Admitting when you don't have all the answers
- Sharing appropriate struggles and challenges
- Asking for help when you need it
- Acknowledging mistakes and learning from them
- Expressing genuine emotions in appropriate ways
- Being open about your growth areas and development needs

Vulnerability is not about oversharing, emotional dumping, or appearing weak. It's about being human in your leadership—real, authentic, and appropriately transparent about your experience.

The Neuroscience of Vulnerable Connection

When someone shares vulnerability appropriately, it triggers the release of oxytocin in both the speaker and the listener. Often called the "bonding hormone," oxytocin promotes trust, empathy, and connection. This neurochemical response explains why vulnerability, far from pushing people away, actually draws them closer.

In my coffee shop conversation, both my colleague and I experienced this oxytocin release. The walls between us came down, and we were able to connect on a much deeper level than we ever had during our professional relationship. He went on to share his own struggles with anxiety and the pressure he felt to always appear strong in his leadership role.

The Vulnerability Paradox in High Achievement

High-achievers face a unique challenge when it comes to vulnerability. The very qualities that drive us to success—perfectionism, self-reliance, competitive instincts—often make vulnerability feel not just uncomfortable but threatening to our identity.

The Armour of Achievement

Success can become a form of armour that protects us from having to be vulnerable. When you're consistently achieving, producing results, and climbing the ladder, it's easy to believe that your worth is tied entirely to your performance. This creates what I call the "armour of achievement"—a protective shell that keeps vulnerability at bay but also keeps authentic connection out.

I have always sought to be an authentic leader. I had a great team and took pride in the fact that people wanted to work with me and share in the challenges we faced. I believe I showed my true self to my team, which helped to build genuine connections and made us stronger together.

The Performance Prison

When your identity becomes fused with your performance, vulnerability feels like a threat to your very sense of self. Admitting struggle, asking for help, or showing uncertainty can feel like you're dismantling the foundation of who you are.

This creates what I call the "performance prison"—a psychological cage where you must constantly achieve, produce, and excel to maintain your sense of worth. The prison walls are made of shoulds and musts, which are rigid rules created from our beliefs:

- I should always have the answers
- I must never appear uncertain
- I should be able to handle anything that comes my way
- I must never let the team see me struggle

The cruel irony is that this prison, designed to protect your reputation and position, actually undermines both. Teams don't need perfect leaders—they need human ones.

The Courage Spectrum: Levels of Vulnerable Leadership

Vulnerability in leadership isn't binary—it exists on a spectrum. Understanding this spectrum can help you practice appropriate vulnerability without crossing into oversharing or emotional dumping.

Level 1: Professional Transparency

This is the entry level of vulnerable leadership and involves being transparent about professional challenges and uncertainties:

- "I'm not sure what the best approach is here. Let me think about it and get back to you."
- "This is outside my area of expertise. Who on the team has experience with this?"
- "I made a mistake in how I handled that situation. Here's what I've learnt."

Even this basic level of transparency can be transformative for leaders who have never shown any uncertainty or admitted any mistakes.

Level 2: Process Sharing

This involves sharing your thinking process, including doubts and considerations:

- "I'm wrestling with this decision. Here's what I'm considering..."
- "I'm feeling uncertain about this direction. Can we explore it together?"

- "This keeps me up at night. How are you feeling about it?"

This level helps team members understand your decision-making process and invites their input in meaningful ways.

Level 3: Emotional Authenticity

This involves sharing appropriate emotions and their impact on your leadership:

- "I'm excited about this opportunity, and I'm also nervous about the risks."
- "I'm disappointed about how this turned out. Let's figure out what we can learn."
- "I'm feeling overwhelmed by everything on our plate. I need to step back and prioritise."

This level creates emotional connection and models emotional intelligence for your team.

Level 4: Personal Integration

This involves sharing how personal experiences inform your professional perspective:

- "My experience with... has taught me the importance of..."
- "I've been in a similar situation, and here's what I wish I'd known..."
- "This reminds me of something I went through. Let me share what I learnt."

This level creates deeper trust and demonstrates that you see team members as whole people, not just professional resources.

The Business Case for Vulnerable Leadership

Whilst the psychological and relational benefits of vulnerability are compelling, the business case is equally strong. Vulnerable leadership creates measurable improvements in team performance, innovation, and organisational health.

Psychological Safety and Performance

Google's Project Aristotle, a comprehensive study of what makes teams effective, identified psychological safety as the number one factor in high-performing teams. Psychological safety—the belief that you can speak up, make mistakes, and be vulnerable without negative consequences—is directly created by vulnerable leadership.

When leaders model vulnerability appropriately, they give permission for others to:

- Share ideas without fear of ridicule
- Admit mistakes before they become crises
- Ask questions without appearing incompetent
- Take reasonable risks without fear of blame
- Provide honest feedback without fear of retaliation

Teams with high psychological safety consistently outperform those without it across every metric: innovation, problem-solving, learning from failure, and overall performance.

Trust and Authentic Influence

Traditional leadership often relies on positional power—the authority that comes with title and role. Vulnerable leadership builds authentic influence—the power that comes from genuine connection and trust.

When I began practising vulnerability, I noticed immediate changes:
- Team members began coming to me with problems earlier, when they were easier to solve
- Innovation increased because people felt safe to share unconventional ideas
- Conflicts were resolved more quickly because people trusted my judgement
- Delegation became more effective because team members understood my reasoning
- Turnover decreased because people felt valued as whole humans, not just workers

Innovation Through Imperfection

Innovation requires experimentation, and experimentation requires comfort with failure. Organisations led by vulnerable leaders are more innovative because they create cultures where imperfection is acceptable and learning from failure is expected.

When leaders hide their mistakes and present only polished successes, they create environments where team members do the same. This kills innovation because it makes experimentation feel too risky.

Overcoming the Fear of Vulnerability

Despite the compelling case for vulnerable leadership, most high achievers still struggle with fear when it comes to being open and authentic. These fears are understandable and can be addressed systematically.

Fear of Being Judged

The fear that others will judge you harshly for showing vulnerability is perhaps the most common barrier. This fear is often based on projection—you assume others will judge you as harshly as you judge yourself.

Reality Check: Most people are far more focused on their own challenges than they are on judging yours. When you share vulnerability appropriately, the typical response is relief and connection, not judgement.

Practice: Start small with low-stakes vulnerability. Notice that the feared judgement rarely materialises, and when it does, it says more about the other person than about you.

Fear of Losing Respect

Many leaders worry that showing vulnerability will undermine their authority or cause team members to lose confidence in their leadership.

Reality Check: Research consistently shows the opposite. Leaders who show appropriate vulnerability are seen as more trustworthy, more human, and more effective. Respect increases rather than decreases.

Practice: Distinguish between vulnerability and incompetence. Saying "I don't know the answer, but I'll find out" maintains authority whilst showing humanity. Saying "I have no idea what I'm doing" without a plan does not.

Fear of Being Taken Advantage Of

Some leaders worry that vulnerability will be seen as weakness and that others will exploit their openness.

Reality Check: Vulnerable leadership, when practised appropriately, actually creates more loyalty and support, not less. People are more likely to protect and support leaders they see as human and authentic.

Practice: Set appropriate boundaries around your vulnerability. Share struggles and uncertainties, but always within the context of your commitment to finding solutions and moving forward.

Practical Strategies for Developing Vulnerable Leadership

Developing comfort with vulnerability is a skill that can be practised and improved. Here are specific strategies for building this capacity:

The Graduated Exposure Approach

Start with low-risk vulnerability and gradually increase as you build confidence:

Week 1: Share one thing you're learning about or one area where you're developing skills

Week 2: Admit when you don't know something, but commit to finding out

Week 3: Share a mistake you made and what you learnt from it

Week 4: Express an emotion (excitement, concern, hope) about a work situation

The Vulnerability Check-In

Before important interactions, ask yourself:

- What would authentic transparency look like in this situation?
- What am I tempted to hide or present differently?
- How can I be more real whilst still being professional?
- What would serve the relationship and the work?

The Learning Leader Stance

Position yourself as someone who is constantly learning rather than someone who already knows everything:

- "I'm curious about..."
- "I'm learning that..."
- "I wonder if..."
- "Help me understand..."

This stance makes vulnerability natural because learning requires admitting what you don't yet know.

Creating Psychologically Safe Environments

Vulnerable leadership isn't just about your own behaviour—it's about creating environments where others feel safe to be vulnerable as well.

Modelling vs. Expecting

The key is to model vulnerability without expecting or demanding it from others. When you share appropriately, you give others permission to do the same, but you don't pressure them.

Signs that you're creating psychological safety:
- People admit mistakes without prompting
- Team members ask questions freely
- Conflicts are addressed directly rather than avoided
- People share ideas even when they're not fully formed
- Team members come to you with problems early

Responding to Others' Vulnerability

How you respond when others are vulnerable is crucial for creating psychological safety:

Do:
- Listen without interrupting
- Thank people for sharing
- Ask how you can support them
- Share your own related experiences if appropriate
- Focus on solutions rather than blame

Don't:
- Immediately jump to advice or solutions
- Minimise their experience
- Use their vulnerability against them later
- Share their personal information with others

- Make it about your own similar experience

The Vulnerability Practices That Transformed My Leadership

The Weekly Team Check-In

I started each team meeting with a brief personal check-in where I shared how I was feeling about our current challenges and what was on my mind. This wasn't therapy or oversharing—it was simply being human about the work we were doing together.

Examples:

- "I'm excited about the progress we're making on this project, and I'm also aware that I'm pushing quite hard because I'm anxious about the deadline."
- "I've been thinking a lot about the feedback from last quarter, and I'm wondering if we need to adjust our approach."
- "I made a mistake in how I communicated that decision last week. I was stressed about other things and didn't explain my reasoning clearly."

The impact was immediate. Team members began sharing their own concerns and insights more freely. Problems surfaced earlier. Solutions emerged from unexpected places because people felt safe to contribute.

The "Learning Moments" Practice

Instead of hiding mistakes or presenting only polished successes, I started regularly sharing "learning moments"—

situations where things didn't go as planned and what we could all learn from them.

This practice had several benefits:
- It normalised failure as part of learning
- It demonstrated that mistakes weren't career-ending
- It created a database of institutional knowledge
- It showed that I valued growth over perfection

The Support Request Protocol

Perhaps the most difficult but transformative practice was learning to ask for help explicitly. As leaders, we're conditioned to be the ones providing support, not requesting it. But asking for help is one of the most powerful forms of vulnerability.

I developed a simple protocol:

1. Identify what I needed help with
2. Be specific about the type of support I was seeking (advice, brainstorming, emotional support, practical assistance)
3. Ask directly rather than hinting or hoping someone would offer
4. Express genuine gratitude for the help received

This practice not only got me the support I needed but also modelled for my team that asking for help was a sign of strength, not weakness.

Vulnerability in Different Leadership Contexts

Vulnerability looks different depending on the context and relationship. Understanding these nuances is crucial for practising appropriate vulnerability.

With Your Team

Vulnerability with your direct reports involves being human about the challenges of leadership, whilst maintaining appropriate authority and direction.

Appropriate:
- Sharing your thinking process on difficult decisions
- Admitting when you're unsure about the best path forward
- Acknowledging the emotional impact of organisational changes
- Being honest about your learning areas and development goals

Inappropriate:
- Sharing personal relationship problems
- Expressing despair or hopelessness about the business
- Using team members as therapists for your personal issues
- Undermining confidence in your ability to lead

With Your Peers

Vulnerability with fellow leaders often involves sharing the unique challenges and pressures of your role.

Appropriate:
- Discussing the loneliness or isolation of leadership
- Sharing strategies for managing stress and pressure
- Admitting areas where you need to develop skills
- Seeking advice on difficult leadership situations

Inappropriate:
- Gossiping about team members or other colleagues
- Sharing confidential business information inappropriately
- Using peer relationships to avoid accountability
- Creating drama or unnecessary competition

With Your Superiors

Vulnerability with bosses or board members requires a careful balance between honesty and confidence.

Appropriate:
- Sharing challenges you're facing and your plans to address them
- Asking for guidance on complex decisions
- Being honest about resource needs or timeline concerns
- Admitting mistakes and showing what you've learnt

Inappropriate:
- Appearing unprepared or incompetent
- Sharing problems without proposed solutions
- Making excuses rather than taking responsibility
- Undermining confidence in your ability to handle the role

The Cultural Shift: From Heroic to Human Leadership

The move towards vulnerable leadership represents a fundamental shift from what I call "heroic leadership" to "human leadership."

Heroic Leadership Characteristics:

- Leader as infallible problem-solver
- Emphasis on individual strength and capability
- Culture of perfectionism and risk avoidance
- Limited psychological safety
- High stress and burnout rates
- Innovation stifled by fear of failure

Human Leadership Characteristics:

- Leader as authentic guide and learner
- Emphasis on collective capability and growth
- Culture of learning and reasonable risk-taking
- High psychological safety
- Sustainable performance and wellbeing
- Innovation encouraged through safe failure

This shift doesn't happen overnight, and it requires courage from leaders who are willing to go first, to model the behaviour they want to see, and to create environments where humanity is valued alongside performance.

Measuring the Impact of Vulnerable Leadership

How do you know if your vulnerable leadership is working? Here are key indicators to watch for:

Team-Level Indicators:

- Increased frequency of early problem reporting
- More questions and clarification requests
- Higher levels of creative and innovative thinking
- Faster resolution of conflicts and misunderstandings
- Decreased turnover and increased engagement
- More cross-functional collaboration

Organisational Indicators:

- Improved customer satisfaction (teams that feel safe often provide better service)
- Faster learning from failures and setbacks
- Increased adaptability to change
- Higher levels of employee engagement and satisfaction
- Improved reputation as an employer
- Better financial performance over time

Personal Indicators:

- Decreased feelings of isolation and pressure
- Increased authentic connections with colleagues
- Greater sense of purpose and meaning in work
- Reduced stress and improved well-being
- More sustainable leadership practices

- Enhanced influence and respect

The Vulnerability Assessment

Use this assessment to evaluate your current relationship with vulnerability in leadership:

Rate each statement from 1 (never) to 5 (always):

1. I admit when I don't know something rather than pretending I do
2. I share my thinking process, including doubts and considerations
3. I acknowledge my mistakes openly and discuss what I've learnt
4. I ask for help when I need it rather than struggling alone
5. I express appropriate emotions about work situations
6. I create environments where others feel safe to be vulnerable
7. I respond supportively when others share struggles or uncertainties
8. I model learning and growth rather than presenting only finished competence
9. I set appropriate boundaries around my vulnerability
10. I prioritise authentic connection alongside professional performance

Scoring:
- 40-50: Strong vulnerable leadership
- 30-39: Developing vulnerable leadership

- 20-29: Limited vulnerable leadership
- Below 20: Opportunity for significant growth

Common Pitfalls and How to Avoid Them

As you develop vulnerable leadership skills, be aware of these common mistakes:

Oversharing or Emotional Dumping

The Mistake: Sharing too much personal information or using professional relationships for emotional support inappropriately.

The Solution: Always ask yourself, "Is this serving the work and the relationship, or is this serving my need to be heard?" Share struggles in the context of professional growth and problem-solving.

Vulnerability Without Boundaries

The Mistake: Being open about everything without considering what's appropriate for the relationship and context.

The Solution: Develop clear boundaries about what you will and won't share in different contexts. Vulnerability should always be purposeful and appropriate.

Using Vulnerability to Avoid Accountability

The Mistake: Sharing struggles as a way to excuse poor performance or avoid taking responsibility.

The Solution: Pair vulnerability with ownership and action. Share challenges alongside your commitment to addressing them.

Expecting Reciprocal Vulnerability

The Mistake: Sharing vulnerability with the expectation that others will do the same, then feeling disappointed when they don't.

The Solution: Practice vulnerability as a gift to the relationship, not as a transaction. Others will respond in their own time and way.

Building Organisational Cultures of Courage

Vulnerable leadership isn't just an individual practice—it's about creating organisational cultures where courage and authenticity are valued alongside competence and performance.

Policy and Practice Alignment

Ensure that your organisational policies support vulnerable leadership:

- Performance reviews that value learning from failure
- Meeting structures that encourage questions and uncertainty
- Communication norms that support directness and honesty
- Conflict resolution processes that address issues directly
- Leadership development programmes that include vulnerability training

Storytelling and Culture Building

Use storytelling to reinforce the value of vulnerability:

- Share stories of times when vulnerability led to better outcomes
- Celebrate examples of team members taking appropriate risks
- Document and share lessons learnt from failures and setbacks

- Highlight innovations that emerged from admitting uncertainty
- Create forums for sharing learning moments and growth experiences

The Ripple Effects of Courageous Leadership

When leaders practice vulnerability courageously, the effects ripple throughout the organisation and beyond:

For Teams: Increased trust, better communication, higher performance, greater innovation, improved well-being

For Organisations: Better culture, increased adaptability, improved reputation, stronger results, more sustainable success

For Industries: Cultural shift towards more human and sustainable business practices

For Society: Modelling of authentic leadership that values both performance and humanity

I've learnt that vulnerability isn't a destination—it's a journey. Each day offers new opportunities to choose courage over comfort, authenticity over armour, connection over control.

The courage to be vulnerable transformed not just my leadership but my entire relationship with success, failure, and human connection. It didn't make leadership easier, but it made it more meaningful, more sustainable, and more effective.

Chapter Summary: Key Takeaways

1. **Vulnerability is strength, not weakness**: Appropriate vulnerability creates trust, psychological safety, and high performance.

2. **Start small and build gradually**: Use the graduated exposure approach to develop comfort with vulnerability over time.

3. **Context matters**: Practice different levels of vulnerability appropriately based on relationships and situations.

4. **Model don't expect**: Create environments where others feel safe to be vulnerable without pressuring them to share.

5. **Boundaries are essential**: Vulnerability without boundaries becomes oversharing and loses its effectiveness.

6. **Measure the impact**: Look for concrete signs that your vulnerable leadership is creating positive changes in your team and organisation.

In our next chapter, we'll explore another critical aspect of healthy leadership: breaking free from co-dependent relationships that drain your energy and undermine your effectiveness.

Chapter 5

Breaking Free from Co-Dependency – Reclaiming Your Power

"You are not required to set yourself on fire to keep someone else warm."

Running a business facing significant challenges means you take on a burden of wanting to succeed for everyone's sake. I somehow felt responsible for everyone else's success, happiness, and well-being. I had become so focused on taking care of others that I had completely neglected taking care of myself.

What people don't realise when they are trapped in a web of co-dependent relationships is how they are slowly drained of energy, their effectiveness is undermined, and how it contributes to their mental health challenges.

Co-dependency is one of the most overlooked but damaging patterns that affect high-achieving leaders. It masquerades as caring, dedication, and a strong work ethic, but underneath lies a more troubling dynamic where your sense of worth becomes tied to your ability to rescue, fix, or care for others at the expense of your own well-being.

Understanding Co-Dependency in a Leadership Context

Co-dependency was originally identified in the context of addiction, describing family members who became obsessed with controlling or fixing their addicted loved one's behaviour. However, the dynamics of co-dependency extend far beyond addiction and are particularly relevant in high-pressure leadership environments.

In a professional context, co-dependency occurs when leaders:

- Feel overly responsible for their team members' performance and well-being
- Struggle to set appropriate boundaries between their role and others' responsibilities
- Experience anxiety or guilt when others are struggling, even when it's not their fault
- Enable poor performance or inappropriate behaviour by not addressing it directly
- Sacrifice their own needs and well-being to meet others' demands
- Derive their sense of worth from being needed and indispensable

The Co-Dependent Leader Profile

Co-dependent leaders often appear to be exceptionally caring and dedicated. They're the ones who stay late to help struggling team members, who take on extra work to prevent others from being overwhelmed, and who seem endlessly available for support and guidance.

These behaviours appear virtuous on the surface, but they create dysfunctional dynamics that ultimately harm both the leader and their team:

For the Leader:
- Chronic exhaustion and burnout
- Resentment towards those they're "helping"
- Loss of personal identity and boundaries
- Inability to focus on strategic priorities
- Deteriorating physical and mental health

For the Team:
- Decreased autonomy and confidence
- Learned helplessness and dependency
- Reduced accountability for their own performance
- Stunted professional growth and development
- Unclear expectations and boundaries

The Origins of Co-Dependent Leadership

Understanding how co-dependent patterns develop can help leaders recognise and address them. These patterns often have deep roots that extend back to childhood experiences and early career conditioning.

Childhood Origins

Many co-dependent leaders were children who took on adult responsibilities early in life. Common backgrounds include:

Parentified Children: Those who became responsible for taking care of parents or siblings emotionally or practically

Peacemakers: Children who felt responsible for managing family conflict and keeping everyone happy

Overachievers: Those who learnt that their worth was tied to their ability to meet others' needs and expectations

Caretakers: Children who grew up with family members who had addiction, mental health issues, or other challenges requiring care.

These early experiences create neural pathways that equate worth with caregiving and that feel anxious when others are struggling or upset.

Professional Conditioning

The business world often reinforces co-dependent tendencies through:

"Servant Leadership" Misunderstanding: Genuine servant leadership involves empowering others; co-dependent leadership involves rescuing them.

Performance Reviews: Rewarding leaders for their team's performance without distinguishing between support and enabling.

Cultural Messages: "Your team's success is your success", taken to unhealthy extremes.

Crisis Management: Environments where leaders are rewarded for jumping in to fix problems rather than developing others' capacity

The Success Trap

Ironically, co-dependent behaviours often lead to short-term success, which reinforces the pattern:

- Teams may perform well when the leader is doing extra work
- Crises get resolved when the leader steps in to fix everything
- People express gratitude for the leader's "dedication"
- Promotions may come as a result of being seen as indispensable

This success creates a feedback loop that makes the co-dependent pattern feel not just normal but necessary.

Recognising Co-Dependent Patterns in Your Leadership

Co-dependency can be difficult to identify because it often looks like good leadership. Here are key signs to watch for:

Emotional Signs:
- Feeling responsible for others' emotions and reactions
- Experiencing anxiety when team members are struggling
- Taking things personally that aren't actually about you
- Feeling guilty when you set boundaries or say no
- Resentment towards those you're "helping"
- Exhaustion that doesn't improve with rest

Behavioural Signs:
- Saying yes to requests even when you're already overwhelmed
- Doing work that others should be doing themselves
- Making excuses for others' poor performance
- Avoiding direct conversations about problems

- Working longer hours to compensate for others
- Being unable to delegate effectively

Relational Signs:
- Team members who seem unable to function without your input
- People coming to you with problems they could solve themselves
- Colleagues who expect you to manage their emotions
- Relationships where you give significantly more than you receive
- Team members who don't take accountability for their own performance

Physical Signs:
- Chronic fatigue that doesn't improve with rest
- Stress-related health issues (headaches, digestive problems, sleep disruption)
- Feeling physically drained after interactions with certain people
- Neglecting your own self-care and health needs

The Neuroscience of Co-Dependency

Understanding what happens in your brain during co-dependent interactions can help you recognise and interrupt these patterns.

The Helper's High

When you help others, your brain releases dopamine and endorphins—the same chemicals involved in addiction. This "helper's high" can become psychologically addictive, leading you to seek out opportunities to rescue or fix others.

The problem arises when this chemical reward becomes your primary source of self-worth and identity. You start to need others to need you, creating a cycle in which you unconsciously foster dependency rather than independence.

The Anxiety Response

Co-dependent individuals often have hyperactive amygdala's that interpret others' distress as their own emergency. When a team member is struggling, your brain may react as if you're personally in danger, triggering fight-or-flight responses that compel you to "fix" the situation.

This neurological response explains why it can feel almost impossible to let others struggle or fail, even when allowing them to do so would be better for their development.

The Boundary Confusion

Co-dependency creates literal confusion in your brain about where you end and others begin. Mirror neurons, which help us empathise with others, can become overactive, causing you to feel others' emotions as if they were your own.

This neural confusion makes it difficult to distinguish between appropriate support and enabling behaviour, between empathy and absorption of others' problems.

The Cost of Co-Dependent Leadership

The price of co-dependent leadership is paid by everyone involved:

Personal Costs:

- **Burnout and Exhaustion**: Constantly taking on others' responsibilities leads to chronic overwhelm
- **Lost Identity**: Your sense of self becomes entirely tied to your role as a helper and fixer
- **Health Problems**: Chronic stress from over-responsibility creates physical and mental health issues
- **Relationship Problems**: Co-dependent patterns often extend to personal relationships
- **Career Stagnation**: Focusing on others' development while neglecting your own

Team Costs:

- **Learned Helplessness**: Team members become dependent rather than developing their own capabilities
- **Reduced Accountability**: People don't take ownership when they know you'll step in
- **Stunted Growth**: Over-protection prevents team members from learning through struggle

- **Resentment**: Some team members may resent being "managed" rather than trusted
- **Poor Performance**: Enabling ultimately leads to lower standards and expectations

Organisational Costs:
- **Scalability Issues**: Organisations can't grow when key leaders are irreplaceable
- **Succession Problems**: Co-dependent leaders don't develop others to take their place
- **Cultural Dysfunction**: Co-dependent dynamics spread throughout the organisation
- **Innovation Stagnation**: People don't take risks when they're used to being rescued
- **Financial Impact**: Inefficiency and poor performance affect the bottom line

Breaking Free: The Recovery Process

Recovering from co-dependent leadership patterns requires both understanding and deliberate practice. It's not about becoming uncaring—it's about caring in healthier, more effective ways.

Step 1: Awareness and Assessment

The first step is honest self-assessment. Use these questions to evaluate your patterns:

Responsibility Assessment:
- Do I feel responsible for my team members' emotions?

- Do I take on work that others should be doing?
- Do I make excuses for others' poor performance?
- Do I feel guilty when I set boundaries?

Boundary Assessment:
- Can I say no without feeling guilty?
- Do I have clear expectations for what others should handle independently?
- Am I able to let others experience natural consequences?
- Do I maintain separate time and space for my own needs?

Identity Assessment:
- Is my self-worth tied to being needed?
- Do I feel valuable when I'm not helping others?
- Can I enjoy relationships where the giving is mutual?
- Do I have interests and goals separate from taking care of others?

Step 2: Boundary Setting

Healthy boundaries are essential for breaking co-dependent patterns. This involves both internal boundaries (what you will and won't feel responsible for) and external boundaries (what you will and won't do for others).

Internal Boundaries:
- I am responsible for my own emotions, not others'
- I can support others without taking on their problems as my own

- Others' struggles are not emergencies I must fix
- People's reactions to my boundaries are not my responsibility

External Boundaries:
- Clear job descriptions and expectations for team members
- Specific processes for when and how you provide support
- Limited availability for non-urgent requests
- Consequences that follow naturally from choices

Boundary Setting in Practice:

Instead of: "Don't worry, I'll handle that presentation for you." Try: "I think we could help you be more confident with presenting. Let's set up some coaching sessions to help you develop them."

Instead of: "I'll stay late to finish this so you can leave on time." Try: "This project is your responsibility. What's your plan for completing it by the deadline?"

Instead of: "I don't want to burden you with this problem." Try: "This falls under your role. I'm confident you can handle it, and I'm here if you need guidance."

Step 3: Emotional Regulation

Co-dependent leaders often struggle with managing their own emotions when others are in distress. Learning to regulate your emotional responses is crucial for maintaining healthy boundaries.

The PAUSE Technique: When you notice the urge to rescue or fix:
- Pause and take a breath

- Acknowledge what you're feeling
- Understand that others' problems aren't your emergencies
- Select a response rather than reacting automatically
- Engage from a place of choice rather than compulsion

The Empathy vs. Absorption Practice:
- Empathy: "I can understand that you're struggling with this project."
- Absorption: "I feel terrible that you're struggling. I must fix this for you."

The goal is to maintain empathy whilst avoiding emotional absorption of others' problems.

Step 4: Redefining Support

Healthy support empowers others rather than creating dependency. This requires a fundamental shift in how you think about helping.

Co-Dependent Support:
- Doing things for others that they can do themselves
- Removing consequences and learning opportunities
- Taking on others' emotions and responsibilities
- Creating dependency rather than independence

Healthy Support:
- Teaching and coaching rather than doing
- Allowing natural consequences whilst providing guidance
- Maintaining emotional boundaries whilst showing care

- Building others' capacity and confidence

Developing Interdependent Leadership

The goal isn't to become an uncaring leader but to develop interdependent relationships where support flows both ways and everyone takes appropriate responsibility.

Characteristics of Interdependent Leadership:

- **Mutual respect**: Trusting others to handle their responsibilities
- **Appropriate boundaries**: Clear about what's yours and what's theirs
- **Shared accountability**: Everyone owns their part of the collective outcomes
- **Developmental focus**: Helping others grow rather than rescuing them
- **Sustainable support**: Caring for others whilst maintaining your own wellbeing

Building Interdependent Teams:

Clear Role Definition: Everyone knows exactly what they're responsible for and what support is available

Regular Check-ins: Scheduled conversations about progress and challenges rather than crisis interventions

Skill Development: Investing in team members' capabilities rather than doing their work for them

Natural Consequences: Allowing people to experience the results of their choices whilst providing appropriate support

Celebration of Independence: Recognising and rewarding self-sufficiency and problem-solving

The Difficult Transition

Changing co-dependent patterns isn't easy. Initially, some team members will struggle with the new boundaries. They will be used to you stepping in to solve their problems, and they will push back when you begin expecting them to handle things independently.

Some relationships may end because of this transition. People who are used to you being endlessly available and accommodating will find the new boundaries uncomfortable. This is painful but necessary.

The Positive Outcomes

During my career as I developed and maintained healthy boundaries and stopped rescuing everyone, remarkable things began to happen:

- Team members developed confidence and skills they never knew they had
- Problems got solved more creatively because people weren't waiting for me to fix everything
- I had energy and time to focus on strategic priorities
- The team became more resilient and adaptable
- My own well-being improved dramatically

Most importantly, I discovered that I could be a caring, supportive leader without sacrificing my own well-being or enabling others' dependency.

Practical Tools for Recovery

Here are specific tools that can help you break free from co-dependent patterns:

The Responsibility Matrix

Create a clear matrix of what is and isn't your responsibility:

Your Responsibility:

- Your own emotions and reactions
- Setting clear expectations and boundaries
- Providing appropriate support and resources
- Making decisions within your authority
- Your own professional development and well-being

Not Your Responsibility:

- Others' emotions and reactions
- Others' job performance (beyond providing support)
- Managing others' relationships or conflicts
- Protecting others from natural consequences
- Others' career development or life choices

The Three Questions Practice

Before stepping in to help or fix, ask yourself:

1. Is this my responsibility or theirs?
2. Will my intervention help them grow or create dependency?
3. Am I acting from care or from my own need to be needed?

The Support Spectrum

Develop a range of support options that promote independence:

Level 1: Emotional support and encouragement

Level 2: Guidance and coaching on approach

Level 3: Resources and tools to solve problems independently

Level 4: Collaborative problem-solving

Level 5: Direct intervention (only in genuine emergencies)

Most situations require Level 1-3 support, not Level 5 intervention.

Maintaining Recovery in High-Pressure Environments

Co-dependent patterns often resurface during times of high stress or crisis. Having strategies to maintain healthy boundaries during these periods is crucial:

Crisis Protocol:

1. Assess whether this is genuinely your crisis to manage
2. Determine what level of support is actually needed
3. Resist the urge to take over completely
4. Maintain boundaries even when others are struggling
5. Take care of your own stress and well-being during the crisis

Regular Boundary Maintenance:

- Weekly review of your responsibilities vs. actions taken
- Monthly assessment of team members' independence and growth
- Quarterly evaluation of your own wellbeing and energy levels

- Annual review of relationship patterns and co-dependent tendencies

The Ripple Effects of Healthy Leadership

When you break free from co-dependent patterns, the positive effects extend far beyond your immediate relationships:

For You:
- Increased energy and well-being
- Greater effectiveness and strategic focus
- Improved relationships both personally and professionally
- Enhanced sense of authentic identity and worth
- Reduced stress and better physical health

For Your Team:
- Increased confidence and capability
- Greater accountability and ownership
- Enhanced problem-solving and innovation
- Improved resilience and adaptability
- Better preparation for leadership roles themselves

For Your Organisation:
- More scalable leadership model
- Stronger succession planning
- Culture of accountability and growth
- Increased innovation and risk-taking
- Better overall performance and sustainability

Chapter Summary: Key Takeaways

1. **Co-dependency masquerades as good leadership**: What looks like dedication and care may actually be unhealthy rescuing and enabling.
2. **Boundaries are essential**: Clear boundaries between your responsibilities and others' protect everyone's wellbeing and growth.
3. **Support should empower, not enable**: Healthy leadership helps others develop capability rather than creating dependency.
4. **Recovery is a process**: Breaking co-dependent patterns takes time, practice, and often involves some relationship difficulties.
5. **Self-care enables better care for others**: Taking care of your own needs allows you to support others more effectively and sustainably.
6. **Interdependence is the goal**: Healthy relationships involve mutual support and shared responsibility rather than one-way caretaking.

In our next chapter, we'll explore how to manage the anxious predictions and limiting beliefs that often drive co-dependent behaviours and other self-defeating patterns.

Chapter 6

Taming the Mind's Predictions - Overcoming Anxious Thoughts and Blocking Beliefs

"You have written the final chapter without reading the book and decided it ends in catastrophe."

This was how Christine described my thinking patterns during one of our early sessions. I had become trapped in a cycle of anxious predictions, constantly imagining the worst possible outcomes and then behaving as if these imagined disasters were inevitable realities.

As a CEO, I found myself lying awake at 3 AM, mentally rehearsing board meetings that might go badly, imagining staff reactions to decisions I hadn't yet made, and predicting catastrophic consequences for choices that were still theoretical. My mind had become a cinema of disasters, playing an endless loop of films where everything went wrong.

What I didn't understand then was that this pattern of anxious prediction wasn't just causing me mental distress—it was actively undermining my leadership effectiveness. When you're constantly preparing for catastrophe, you make decisions from a place of fear rather than wisdom, and you create the very problems you're trying to avoid.

Understanding Anxious Predictions

Anxious predictions are your mind's attempt to prepare for every possible negative outcome. On the surface, this seems logical—if you can anticipate problems, you can prevent them. But anxious predictions are different from healthy contingency planning in crucial ways:

Healthy Planning vs. Anxious Prediction

Healthy Planning:

- Based on a realistic assessment of probabilities
- Focuses on actionable responses to likely scenarios
- Time-limited and solution-oriented
- Reduces anxiety by creating preparedness
- Leads to effective decision-making

Anxious Prediction:

- Based on fear rather than probability
- Focuses on catastrophic outcomes with no solutions
- Endless and rumination-oriented
- Increases anxiety by rehearsing disasters
- Leads to paralysis or panic-driven decisions

The key difference is that healthy planning empowers action, whilst anxious prediction paralyses it.

The Prediction Spiral

Anxious predictions follow a predictable pattern:

1. **Trigger**: Something uncertain or challenging appears

2. **What if**: Your mind starts generating possible negative outcomes
3. **Escalation**: Each "what if" leads to worse possibilities
4. **Catastrophising**: You imagine the worst possible scenario
5. **Emotional flooding**: Fear, anxiety, or panic takes over
6. **Behavioural response**: You either avoid the situation or make fear-based decisions

For me, this spiral often started with unreasonable comments and requests from senior stakeholders. Within minutes, my mind would have constructed elaborate disaster scenarios where I was fired, the company failed, and my career was ruined.

The Neuroscience of Anxious Thinking

Understanding what happens in your brain during anxious prediction can help you recognise and interrupt these patterns.

The Overactive Amygdala

When you're in chronic stress, your amygdala—the brain's alarm system—becomes hypersensitive. It starts interpreting neutral or ambiguous situations as threats, triggering the cascade of anxious predictions.

This hypervigilance evolved to keep our ancestors alive in dangerous environments, but in modern leadership roles, it becomes maladaptive. Your brain treats a challenging executive presentation with the same urgency as a physical threat.

The Underactive Prefrontal Cortex

Chronic anxiety suppresses activity in your prefrontal cortex—the brain region responsible for rational thinking, planning, and perspective-taking. This explains why anxious predictions feel so real and compelling even when they're obviously irrational in hindsight.

When your prefrontal cortex is offline, you lose access to:

- Probability assessment (how likely is this really?)
- Solution generation (what could I do if this happened?)
- Perspective-taking (how important will this be in a year?)
- Self-soothing (I can handle whatever comes up)

The Confirmation Bias Loop

Once you've generated an anxious prediction, your brain starts looking for evidence to support it whilst ignoring evidence that contradicts it. This confirmation bias makes the feared outcome appear ever more likely and unavoidable.

For example, if you predict that a presentation will go badly, you'll notice every potential problem whilst overlooking your preparation, experience, and past successes.

Common Anxious Predictions for Leaders

Different leadership challenges trigger different types of anxious predictions. Recognising these patterns can help you catch them early:

Performance Predictions:

- "This presentation will be a disaster"

- "Everyone will realise I don't know what I'm doing"
- "My performance review will be terrible"

Relationship Predictions:
- "My team will lose respect for me"
- "The board will lose confidence in me"
- "People will think I'm weak/incompetent/unprepared"

Career Predictions:
- "I'll be fired"
- "My career will be ruined"
- "I'll never recover from this mistake"
- "I'll end up unemployed and unsuccessful"

Organisational Predictions:
- "The company will fail"
- "We'll lose our biggest client"
- "The team will fall apart"
- "Everything I've built will be destroyed"

Blocking Beliefs: The Foundation of Anxious Predictions

Underneath anxious predictions lie deeper blocking beliefs—core assumptions about yourself, others, and the world that create the foundation for fearful thinking.

Core Blocking Beliefs for High-Achievers:

About Competence:
- "I'm not as smart/capable as people think I am"
- "I'm always one mistake away from being found out"

- "I don't deserve my success"
- "I'm fooling everyone about my abilities"

About Worth:
- "I'm only valuable when I'm performing well"
- "I must be perfect to be accepted"
- "My worth depends on others' approval"
- "I'm not enough as I am"

About Control:
- "I must control everything to prevent disaster"
- "If I'm not vigilant, everything will fall apart"
- "Other people are unreliable and will let me down"
- "The world is fundamentally dangerous and unpredictable"

About Success:
- "Success is temporary and will be taken away"
- "Good things don't last"
- "I don't deserve to be happy and successful"
- "Success means increased danger and responsibility"

These beliefs operate largely below conscious awareness, but they drive the anxious predictions that plague your thinking.

The Cost of Anxious Predictions

Living in a constant state of anxious prediction creates enormous costs:

Decision-Making Costs:

- **Analysis paralysis**: Over-thinking decisions to avoid imagined catastrophes
- **Risk aversion**: Avoiding necessary risks due to fear of negative outcomes
- **Premature decisions**: Making hasty choices to escape the anxiety of uncertainty
- **Conservative strategies**: Playing it safe instead of pursuing opportunities

Leadership Costs:
- **Reduced confidence**: Second-guessing yourself undermines your authority
- **Communication problems**: Anxiety makes it harder to communicate clearly
- **Team anxiety**: Your anxious energy spreads to your team
- **Missed opportunities**: Fear prevents you from taking advantage of openings

Personal Costs:
- **Chronic stress**: Constant worry creates physical and mental health problems
- **Sleep disruption**: Racing thoughts prevent restorative rest
- **Relationship strain**: Anxiety affects your ability to connect with others
- **Reduced joy**: Constant worry makes it hard to enjoy successes

Cognitive Behavioural Techniques for Anxious Predictions

CBT provides powerful tools for recognising and challenging anxious predictions. These techniques help you engage your rational mind and break the cycle of catastrophic thinking.

The Thought Record Technique

When you notice anxious predictions, use this systematic approach:

1. Situation: What triggered the anxious thinking?

2. Emotion: What are you feeling and how intensely (1-10)?

3. Automatic Thought: What predictions went through your mind?

4. Evidence For: What supports this prediction?

5. Evidence Against: What contradicts this prediction?

6. Balanced Thought: What's a more realistic perspective?

7. New Emotion: How do you feel now (1-10)?

Example:

Situation: Scheduled to present to the board next week

Emotion: Anxiety (8/10)

Automatic Thought: "I'll forget everything and make a complete fool of myself"

Evidence For: I'm nervous about the presentation

Evidence Against: I've given hundreds of successful presentations; I'm well-prepared; forgetting everything has never actually happened

Balanced Thought: "I'm nervous, which is normal. I'm well-prepared and have a track record of successful presentations"

New Emotion: Nervous but confident (4/10)

The Probability Assessment

Most anxious predictions assume that feared outcomes are highly likely when they're quite rare. This exercise helps restore a realistic perspective:

1. **Identify the specific prediction**: Be precise about what you're predicting
2. **Estimate the probability**: What are the actual odds this will happen?
3. **Consider base rates**: How often has this happened to you or others?
4. **Factor in your resources**: What skills, experience, and support do you have?
5. **Reassess the probability**: Given all factors, what's the realistic likelihood?

Example:

Prediction: "I'll be fired after the quarterly review"

Initial probability estimate: 70%

Base rate consideration: I've never been fired; quarterly reviews have generally been positive

Resource consideration: I have a strong performance history, supportive relationships, and valuable skills

Reassessed probability: 5%

The Decatastrophising Technique

This technique helps you work through feared outcomes to reduce their emotional impact:

1. **Identify the worst-case scenario**: What's the absolute worst thing that could happen?
2. **Assess the likelihood**: How probable is this worst-case scenario?
3. **Develop coping strategies**: How would you handle it if it did happen?
4. **Consider partial outcomes**: What less extreme outcomes are more likely?
5. **Focus on response rather than prevention**: What can you control in your response?

Example:

Worst case: "I'll be fired and never find another job"

Likelihood: Very low (less than 1%)

Coping strategies: I have savings, skills, network, and experience; I would update my CV, reach out to contacts, and likely find something within 3-6 months

Partial outcomes: More likely scenarios include feedback for improvement, additional support, or minor role adjustments

Controllable response: I can prepare well, ask for feedback, and maintain good relationships regardless of the outcome

Mindfulness-Based Approaches

Mindfulness techniques help you observe anxious predictions without getting caught up in them.

The Observer Self Practice

When anxious predictions arise:

1. **Notice**: "I'm having the thought that..."
2. **Observe**: Watch the thoughts without judgement
3. **Breathe**: Take several deep breaths to engage your parasympathetic nervous system
4. **Choose**: Decide whether to engage with the thoughts or let them pass

This practice helps you relate to thoughts as mental events rather than facts.

The 5-4-3-2-1 Grounding Technique

When anxious predictions create overwhelming feelings:

- **5 things you can see** in your environment
- **4 things you can touch** around you
- **3 things you can hear** right now
- **2 things you can smell** in this moment
- **1 thing you can taste** currently

This technique pulls your attention away from internal predictions and into present-moment awareness.

The RAIN Technique

When facing difficult, anxious predictions:

- **R**ecognise: What am I experiencing right now?

- **A**llow: Can I let this be here without fighting it?
- **I**nvestigate: What does this feel like in my body?
- **N**urture: What do I need right now to take care of myself?

Challenging Core Blocking Beliefs

Surface-level anxious predictions often stem from deeper blocking beliefs. Addressing these core beliefs creates more lasting change.

Belief Identification Techniques

The Downward Arrow Technique: Start with an anxious prediction and keep asking, "What would that mean about me?" until you reach the core belief.

Example: "I'll fail at this presentation" ↓

What would that mean about me? "I'm not good at my job" ↓

What would that mean about me? "I'm not competent enough for this role" ↓

What would that mean about me? "I'm fundamentally inadequate" ← Core belief

The Pattern Recognition Exercise: Look for themes across your anxious predictions:

- Do they all involve being judged or rejected?
- Do they focus on loss of control or safety?
- Do they centre on competence or worth?
- Do they involve abandonment or isolation?

Belief Challenging Process

Once you've identified core blocking beliefs, challenge them systematically:

1. Evidence Examination:
- What evidence supports this belief?
- What evidence contradicts it?
- Would this evidence convince an impartial observer?

2. Origin Exploration:
- Where did this belief come from?
- Was it true when it was formed?
- Is it still true now?

3. Alternative Development:
- What would be a more balanced belief?
- What would you tell a friend with this belief?
- What belief would be more helpful and realistic?

4. Behavioural Testing:
- How can you test the new belief through action?
- What small experiments can you try?
- What evidence would convince you that the new belief is true?

Practical Tools for Daily Use

Here are specific tools you can use when anxious predictions arise:

The STOP Method

Stop what you're doing

Take three deep breaths

Observe your thoughts without judgement

Proceed with conscious choice rather than automatic reaction

The Worry Window

Set aside 15 minutes daily for "worry time":

- When anxious predictions arise during the day, note them and defer to worry time
- During worry time, examine each worry systematically
- Distinguish between productive planning and unproductive rumination
- End worry time decisively and return to present-moment activities

The Action vs. Worry Matrix

For each anxious prediction, ask:

- Is this something I can take action on?
- Is worrying about it helpful or harmful?

Actionable + Helpful worry: Make a plan and take steps

Actionable + Unhelpful worry: Make a plan and stop ruminating

Not actionable + Helpful worry: Accept uncertainty and focus on what you can control

Not actionable + Unhelpful worry: Practice letting go and mindful acceptance

My Journey with Anxious Predictions

Looking back, I can see how anxious predictions have been a part of me for a long time. They have impacted me in many areas of my life. I was living in a constant state of mental rehearsal for disasters that never came. My mind had become a writer's room for tragedy, constantly scripting scenarios where everything went wrong.

The turning point came when Christine helped me see the difference between healthy planning and anxious prediction. She taught me to ask: "Is this thought helping me prepare, or is it just torturing me?"

The Homework Assignment

Christine gave me a homework assignment that changed my relationship with anxious predictions: for one week, I had to write down every anxious prediction I noticed and then track what actually happened.

The results were eye-opening:

- 95% of my anxious predictions never came true
- When problems did arise, they were usually different from what I'd predicted
- I handled challenges better than I'd anticipated
- My predictions were almost always more catastrophic than reality

This exercise helped me see that my mind was not a reliable fortune-teller and that I could handle whatever occurred.

Learning to Live with Uncertainty

The hardest part of recovery was learning to tolerate uncertainty without immediately generating anxious predictions. I had to practice sitting with "I don't know" without filling the void with catastrophic scenarios.

Techniques that helped:

- Regular mindfulness meditation to build tolerance for uncertainty
- Focusing on present-moment actions rather than future outcomes
- Developing trust in my ability to handle whatever arose
- Creating support systems for when challenges did occur

Building Resilience Against Anxious Thinking

Rather than trying to eliminate anxious predictions entirely, the goal is to build resilience, so they don't control your decisions or drain your energy.

The Resilience Banking System

Think of resilience as a bank account with deposits and withdrawals:

Deposits (Build resilience):

- Regular sleep and rest
- Physical exercise and movement
- Nutritious eating patterns
- Social connection and support

- Engaging in enjoyable activities
- Mindfulness and meditation practice
- Accomplishing meaningful goals

Withdrawals (Drain resilience):
- Chronic worry and rumination
- Poor sleep or irregular schedule
- Sedentary lifestyle
- Isolation from supportive relationships
- Overwork without breaks
- Ignoring physical and emotional needs
- Focusing only on problems and challenges

The Support Network Activation

When anxious predictions arise:
- Identify trusted advisors who can provide perspective
- Share your concerns with people who know you well
- Ask for feedback on the realism of your predictions
- Seek advice on practical steps you can take
- Accept emotional support without feeling weak

Creating Prediction-Resistant Decisions

Make decisions from a place of wisdom rather than fear by:

The Future Self Technique

When facing decisions influenced by anxious predictions:

1. Imagine yourself five years from now

2. What would that wiser, more experienced version of you choose?
3. What advice would your future self give your current self?
4. What decision would you be proud of in retrospect?

The Deathbed Test

For major decisions, ask yourself:

- On my deathbed, will I regret taking this risk or not taking it?
- What would I tell my children about how to approach this situation?
- What does courage look like here?
- What serves my growth vs. what serves my fear?

Chapter Summary: Key Takeaways

1. **Anxious predictions are different from healthy planning**: One empowers action, whilst the other paralyses it.
2. **Most predictions don't come true**: Your mind is not a reliable fortune-teller, and you can handle more than you think.
3. **Blocking beliefs fuel anxious predictions**: Address core beliefs about competence, worth, control, and success.
4. **CBT techniques provide practical tools**: Thought records, probability assessment, and decatastrophising help restore perspective.

5. **Mindfulness builds resilience**: Learning to observe thoughts without being consumed by them is a crucial skill.
6. **Uncertainty is manageable**: You don't need to predict the future to make good decisions in the present.

In our next chapter, we'll explore how to focus your energy on what you can actually influence whilst releasing what lies beyond your control.

Chapter 7

Control the Controllables - Finding Peace in Uncertainty

"You have power over your mind—not outside events. Realise this, and you will find strength."

— Marcus Aurelius

During the height of my crisis as CEO, I was desperately trying to control everything. I was attempting to manage situations I couldn't influence and losing sleep over decisions that weren't mine to make. I had become like someone trying to steer a ship by gripping the ocean itself rather than the wheel.

The harder I tried to control the uncontrollable, the more out of control I felt. My energy was pulled in a hundred directions, most of them far beyond my influence. I grew exhausted, anxious, and less effective, having completely misunderstood where my real power lay.

The concept of "controlling the controllables" became one of the most transformative frameworks in my recovery. It's deceptively simple but profoundly powerful: focus your energy entirely on what you can influence and consciously release what you cannot.

This isn't about becoming passive or giving up—it's about becoming strategically focused and emotionally free.

Understanding the Control Paradox

High-achievers often struggle with a fundamental paradox: the very qualities that drive success—determination, persistence, high standards—can become liabilities when applied to situations beyond our control.

The Illusion of Control

Modern business culture promotes the illusion that effective leaders can control outcomes through sheer force of will, preparation, and effort. We speak of "owning results," "driving performance," and "making things happen" as if external factors don't exist.

This illusion is reinforced by:

- **Success stories** that focus on individual effort, whilst ignoring luck and timing
- **Performance reviews** that hold leaders accountable for factors beyond their influence
- **Business media** that attributes complex outcomes to single leadership decisions
- **Cultural messaging** that equates leadership with power

The reality is far more complex. Even the most capable leaders operate within systems influenced by market forces, competitor actions, regulatory changes, economic cycles, and countless other variables outside their direct control.

The Control Addiction

Many executives become addicted to control because it provides temporary relief from anxiety about uncertainty. When we feel like we're managing every variable, we experience a brief sense of security and competence.

But this addiction creates a vicious cycle:

1. **Anxiety** about uncertain outcomes
2. **Attempt to control** more variables
3. **Temporary relief** from feeling "in charge"
4. **Increased anxiety** when control inevitably fails
5. **Escalated attempts** to control even more

The end result is leaders who are simultaneously overcontrolling and under-effective, micromanaging details whilst missing strategic opportunities.

The Stoic Framework: What You Can and Cannot Control

The ancient Stoic philosophers developed perhaps the most practical framework for understanding control. They divided all concerns into three categories:

Category 1: Complete Control

These are things entirely within your power:

- Your thoughts and interpretations
- Your decisions and choices
- Your actions and responses
- Your effort and preparation

- Your values and character
- Your attention and focus

Category 2: Some Influence

These are things you can influence but not completely control:

- Your team's performance
- Customer satisfaction
- Relationships with colleagues
- Your reputation
- Business results
- Market position

Category 3: No Control

These are things completely outside your power:

- Other people's decisions
- Market conditions
- Regulatory changes
- Natural disasters
- Competitor actions
- Past events
- Other people's opinions

The Stoic principle: Focus completely on Category 1, influence Category 2 through your Category 1 actions, and accept Category 3 with equanimity.

The Neuroscience of Control and Letting Go

Understanding what happens in your brain during attempts to control can help you recognise when you're fighting unwinnable battles.

The Control Centre: Prefrontal Cortex

Your prefrontal cortex manages executive functions, including planning, decision-making, and emotional regulation. When you focus on what you can control, this region operates efficiently and effectively.

However, when you try to control uncontrollable factors, your prefrontal cortex becomes overloaded, leading to:

- Decision fatigue from too many variables
- Analysis paralysis from overwhelming complexity
- Emotional dysregulation from constant frustration
- Decreased creativity and strategic thinking

The Stress Response to Lack of Control

When you feel out of control, your amygdala triggers stress responses designed for physical threats. This creates a cascade of stress hormones that:

- Narrow your attention to immediate threats
- Reduce your ability to see big-picture solutions
- Increase emotional reactivity
- Impair memory and learning
- Compromised immune function and physical health

The Neurochemistry of Letting Go

When you successfully let go of uncontrollables, your brain releases calming neurotransmitters:

- **GABA** reduces anxiety and promotes relaxation
- **Serotonin** improves mood and emotional stability
- **Dopamine** increases motivation and focus
- **Endorphins** create feelings of well-being and peace

This neurochemical shift doesn't just feel better—it makes you more effective at influencing what you actually can control.

Practical Tools for Identifying Controllables

The first step in applying this framework is clearly identifying what falls into each category for your specific situation.

The Control Audit

For any situation causing you stress, create three columns:

Column 1: I Can Control

- My preparation and effort
- My response to setbacks
- My communication and attitude
- My decisions and priorities
- My learning and development

Column 2: I Can Influence

- Team performance through coaching and support
- Customer relationships through service and value
- Market position through strategic choices

- Stakeholder opinions through consistent action
- Business results through focused effort

Column 3: I Cannot Control

- Economic conditions
- Competitor strategies
- Regulatory changes
- Other people's decisions
- Past mistakes or missed opportunities

The Energy Allocation Exercise

Track where you're spending mental and emotional energy:

1. **List your current concerns** and stressors
2. **Categorise each** as controllable, influenceable, or uncontrollable
3. **Estimate the percentage** of energy you're spending on each category
4. **Identify misallocations** where you're focusing on uncontrollables
5. **Create a reallocation plan** to shift energy towards controllables

Most stressed leaders discover they're spending 60-80% of their energy on uncontrollables whilst neglecting areas where they have real power.

The Art of Strategic Letting Go

Letting go doesn't mean giving up—it means strategically releasing energy from unproductive focuses so you can invest it where it matters most.

What Letting Go Looks Like in Practice

Instead of: Obsessing over a competitor's new product launch, **Try**: Focusing on how to make your own products better

Instead of: Worrying about economic uncertainty, **Try**: Building resilience and adaptability in your business model

Instead of: Trying to control a difficult board member's behaviour, **Try**: Preparing excellent presentations and clear communication

Instead of: Stressing about team members' personal problems, **Try**: Providing appropriate support whilst maintaining boundaries

The Letting Go Process

When you notice yourself trying to control the uncontrollable:

1. **Pause**: Stop and take three deep breaths
2. **Recognise**: "I'm trying to control something outside my power"
3. **Redirect**: "What can I actually influence in this situation?"
4. **Act**: Take one concrete step within your control
5. **Release**: Consciously let go of the uncontrollable elements

This process trains your brain to automatically redirect from unproductive worry to productive action.

Focusing on Your Circle of Influence

Stephen Covey's concept of the Circle of Influence provides a powerful framework for strategic focus.

Your Circle of Concern

These are all the things you care about but may not be able to directly influence: global economy, company stock price, industry trends, competitor actions, and regulatory environment.

Your Circle of Influence

These are things you care about and can directly influence: your team's performance, customer relationships, personal skills, strategic decisions, and communication effectiveness.

The principle: Reactive people focus on their Circle of Concern and feel increasingly powerless. Proactive people focus on their Circle of Influence and gradually expand it through effective action.

Expanding Your Circle of Influence

As you focus consistently on what you can control and influence:

- Your competence and credibility increase
- Others begin to seek your input on broader issues
- Your formal authority may expand
- Your informal influence definitely grows
- Your Circle of Influence naturally enlarges

This expansion happens not through force or manipulation but through demonstrated effectiveness in areas within your control.

Emotional Regulation and Acceptance

Controlling the controllables isn't just about action—it's about emotional regulation and the practice of acceptance.

The Acceptance Paradox

Acceptance doesn't mean passive resignation—it means clear-eyed recognition of reality as the starting point for effective action. When you stop fighting reality, you can engage with it more skillfully.

Resistance looks like:

- "This shouldn't be happening"
- "I can't believe they did that"
- "It's not fair that..."
- "If only things were different..."

Acceptance looks like:

- "This is what's happening right now"
- "Given this reality, what's my best response?"
- "I don't like this situation, but I can work with it"
- "What can I learn or gain from this challenge?"

The RAIN Practice for Difficult Situations

When facing uncontrollable circumstances:

Recognise: What is actually happening right now?

Allow: Can I let this situation be what it is without fighting it?

Investigate: What am I feeling, and what do I need?

Non-identification: This situation is not me; it's something I'm experiencing

This practice helps you respond from wisdom rather than reactivity.

Decision-Making Through the Control Lens

Using the controllables framework transforms how you approach decisions and problem-solving.

The Control-Based Decision Process

For any decision:

1. **Clarify what you're actually deciding**: Focus on choices truly within your power
2. **Identify your controllable factors**: What inputs, efforts, and responses can you manage?
3. **Acknowledge the uncontrollables**: What external factors might influence outcomes?
4. **Make decisions based on controllables**: Choose based on what you can actually manage.
5. **Prepare to adapt**: Plan how you'll respond to uncontrollable changes

Example: Launching a New Product

Traditional approach: Try to predict market response, competitor reactions, economic conditions, and customer adoption rates

Control-focused approach:

- Focus on product quality, marketing message, team preparation, and launch execution
- Acknowledge that market response and competitor actions are unknowable
- Plan multiple scenarios for different receptions
- Commit fully to excellent execution whilst remaining flexible about outcomes

Building Organisational Cultures of Strategic Focus

Leaders who master the controllables create organisational cultures that are both focused and resilient.

Cultural Characteristics

Teams that focus on controllables demonstrate:

- **Clear accountability** for what they can actually influence
- **Reduced blame** and increased problem-solving
- **Higher innovation** because energy isn't wasted on worry
- **Better adaptability** when uncontrollable changes occur
- **Lower stress** and higher satisfaction
- **More strategic thinking** and fewer reactive decisions

Practical Implementation

In team meetings: Start with what you can control and influence before discussing external challenges

In performance reviews: Evaluate people on effort, decisions, and responses rather than outcomes alone

In strategic planning: Distinguish between assumptions (uncontrollable) and commitments (controllable)

In crisis management: Focus first on your response capabilities before analysing external factors

My Personal Journey with Control

Looking back at my breakdown, I can see clearly how my attempts to control the uncontrollable contributed to my crisis. I was trying to manage: The parent company's leadership transitions and resulting strategic shifts, External market conditions affecting our competitive position, and Senior stakeholders' evolving priorities

Meanwhile, I was neglecting areas where I had real control:

- My own stress management and well-being
- Clear communication about realistic expectations
- Building resilience into our business model
- My own decision-making processes

The Turning Point

The breakthrough came when Christine asked me to list everything I was worried about and then categorise each item as controllable or uncontrollable. The exercise was shocking—over 80% of my mental energy was focused on things completely outside my influence.

She then asked: "What would happen if you spent that 80% of energy on the 20% you can actually control?"

The answer was obvious but revolutionary: I would be far more effective and significantly less stressed.

The Practical Application

I began implementing the controllables framework systematically:

Daily Practice: Each morning, I identified the three most important things within my control for that day

Weekly Review: I assessed whether my energy allocation matched my actual influence

Monthly Reset: I consciously released concerns that had proven to be outside my control

Crisis Response: During difficult situations, I immediately categorised factors and focused on my response

The results were transformative. My stress levels decreased dramatically by focusing on what I could control.

Advanced Practices for Mastery

Once you've grasped the basic framework, these advanced practices can deepen your mastery:

The Influence Mapping Exercise

For complex situations, create a visual map:

1. Put the situation or outcome in the centre
2. Draw concentric circles around it, representing levels of influence
3. Place factors in appropriate circles based on your actual control
4. Focus your energy on inner circles whilst monitoring outer ones

The Control Journal

Keep a weekly journal tracking:

- Situations where you tried to control the uncontrollable
- Energy wasted on unproductive worry
- Moments when focusing on controllables led to better outcomes
- Lessons learned about where your real power lies

The Serenity Practice

Adapt the famous Serenity Prayer for leadership: "Grant me the serenity to accept what I cannot control, the courage to change what I can, and the wisdom to know the difference."

Make this a daily reflection.

Dealing with Setbacks and Uncontrollable Events

Even when you focus on controllables, uncontrollable events will still occur. The framework helps you respond more effectively when they do.

The Response Protocol

When uncontrollable negative events occur:

1. **Feel the emotions**: Don't suppress natural reactions to disappointment or frustration
2. **Assess the damage**: Understand what actually happened vs. what you feared
3. **Identify your choices**: What options do you have in response?
4. **Focus on learning**: What can this experience teach you?

5. **Plan your response**: How will you move forward given this new reality?

Building Antifragility

Nassim Taleb's concept of antifragility—systems that get stronger from stress—applies perfectly to the controllables framework. When you consistently focus on what you can control, you become more resilient and capable over time.

Fragile: Broken by uncontrollable events

Resilient: Survives uncontrollable events

Antifragile: Grows stronger from uncontrollable events

Leaders who master the controllables develop antifragility because they're constantly building capabilities, relationships, and systems rather than just managing crises.

Chapter Summary: Key Takeaways

1. **Energy allocation determines effectiveness**: Where you focus your mental and emotional energy determines your impact and stress levels.

2. **Control is largely an illusion**: Most outcomes depend on factors beyond your direct control, but your response is always within your power.

3. **Categories matter**: Clearly distinguishing between what you can control, influence, and must accept is crucial for strategic focus.

4. **Letting go increases power**: Releasing uncontrollables frees energy for areas where you can make a real difference.

5. **Focus expands influence**: Consistently demonstrating effectiveness in your Circle of Influence naturally expands it over time.
6. **Response is always controllable**: Regardless of what happens to you, how you respond is always within your power.

In our next chapter, we'll explore how to anchor yourself in the present moment whilst building the mindfulness skills that make controlling the controllables possible.

Chapter 8
The Power of Now - Living in the Present Moment

"The present moment is the only time over which we have dominion."

— Thich Nhat Hanh

Three months into my recovery, I noticed how much more aware I was of everyday events we take for granted. This could be noticing the weather and the noise the wind was making, or it could be the taste of the food I was eating, rather than rushing through my lunch whilst sitting at my desk.

This moment of simple awareness marked a profound shift in my recovery. For years, I had been living entirely in my head—planning the next meeting whilst in the current one, solving tomorrow's problems during today's conversations, and missing the richness of immediate experience in favour of mental time travel to futures that rarely unfolded as expected.

Learning to live in the present moment wasn't just a relaxation technique—it became the foundation for clear thinking, effective decision-making, and sustainable leadership. When you're fully present, you have access to your complete intelligence rather than the fragmented attention that characterises most executive thinking.

Understanding Present-Moment Awareness

Present-moment awareness isn't about emptying your mind or attaining some mystical state. It's about training your attention to engage fully with whatever you're experiencing right now, rather than splitting your consciousness between multiple time zones and imagined scenarios.

The Three States of Consciousness

Most people operate in one of three states:

Past-Focused: Replaying events, analysing mistakes, nostalgic thinking, regret, resentment.

Future-Focused: Planning scenarios, worrying about outcomes, anticipating problems, goal-oriented thinking.

Present-Aware: Engaging with current experience, responsive rather than reactive, clear perception of reality.

All three states have their place, but most high-achievers spend 90% of their time in past and future states, missing the only moment where they can actually take effective action.

The Present-Moment Paradox for Leaders

High-achieving leaders often resist present-moment practices because they seem to conflict with the demands of strategic thinking and long-term planning. This creates a paradox:

- You believe you need to constantly think about the future to be an effective leader
- But the quality of your future depends entirely on the quality of your present-moment decisions and actions

- The more you scatter your attention across multiple time frames, the less effective you become in any of them

The resolution is understanding that present-moment awareness enhances rather than diminishes strategic capability.

The Neuroscience of Presence

Understanding what happens in your brain during present-moment awareness can help you appreciate its practical benefits for leadership.

The Default Mode Network

When your mind isn't focused on specific tasks, it defaults to what neuroscientists call the Default Mode Network (DMN)—a network of brain regions that become active during rest. For most people, the DMN is dominated by:

- Rumination about past events
- Worry about future scenarios
- Self-referential thinking ("What does this mean about me?")
- Mental wandering and distraction

In high-stress individuals, the DMN can become a source of chronic anxiety and scattered attention.

The Executive Attention Network

Present-moment awareness activates your Executive Attention Network—brain regions responsible for:

- Focused attention and concentration
- Cognitive flexibility and adaptability
- Working memory and information processing

- Emotional regulation and self-control

When this network is engaged, you have access to your full cognitive capacity rather than the diminished thinking that comes with scattered attention.

The Neuroplasticity of Mindfulness

Regular present-moment practice literally changes your brain structure:

- **Increased cortical thickness** in areas related to attention and emotional processing
- **Reduced amygdala reactivity,** leading to less stress and anxiety
- **Enhanced connectivity** between the prefrontal cortex and emotional centres
- **Improved default mode network regulation,** reducing mental wandering and rumination

These changes aren't just subjective improvements—they're measurable enhancements to cognitive function.

The Business Case for Present-Moment Awareness

Beyond personal well-being, present-moment awareness creates measurable improvements in leadership effectiveness.

Enhanced Decision-Making

When you're fully present during decision-making:

- You have access to more complete information about the current situation

- You can read non-verbal cues and subtle dynamics in meetings
- Your intuition and experience can inform your choices
- You're less likely to make reactive decisions based on anxiety or pressure
- You can distinguish between urgent and important priorities more clearly

Research from Harvard Business School shows that leaders who practice mindfulness make significantly better strategic decisions and are more effective at managing complex situations.

Improved Communication and Relationships

Present-moment awareness revolutionises your ability to connect with others:

- **Active listening**: You hear not just words but tone, emotion, and underlying concerns
- **Empathetic response**: You can sense what others need and respond appropriately
- **Conflict resolution**: You remain calm and creative during difficult conversations
- **Team dynamics**: You notice patterns and undercurrents that affect group performance
- **Authentic presence**: People feel truly seen and heard in your interactions

Increased Innovation and Creativity

When your mind isn't constantly racing between past and future, you create space for:

- Novel connections between disparate ideas
- Insights that emerge from quiet reflection
- Creative solutions to complex problems
- Recognition of opportunities others might miss
- Fresh perspectives on persistent challenges

Many breakthrough innovations come not from intense mental effort but from moments of present-moment clarity.

Common Obstacles to Present-Moment Awareness

High-achievers face specific challenges when trying to develop present-moment awareness:

The Productivity Paradox

The belief: "I'm too busy to be present; I need to keep thinking ahead"

The reality: Present-moment awareness makes you more productive, not less

When you're fully engaged with current tasks, you complete them more efficiently and effectively than when your attention is divided.

The Control Illusion

The belief: "If I stop thinking about future problems, they won't get solved"

The reality: Most problems are better solved through focused, present-moment thinking than anxious rumination

Present moment awareness allows you to engage with challenges when you have the capacity to address them effectively.

The Professional Identity Crisis

The belief: "Mindfulness is soft and doesn't belong in business"

The reality: Present-moment awareness is a performance enhancement tool, not a relaxation technique

Companies like Google, Goldman Sachs, and General Mills have implemented mindfulness programs because they improve bottom-line results.

Practical Techniques for Developing Present-Moment Awareness

Here are specific practices tailored for busy executives:

The Micro-Meditation Practice

You don't need hours of meditation to develop present-moment awareness. These micro-practices can be done throughout your day:

The Three-Breath Reset: Between meetings, take three conscious breaths, focusing entirely on the sensation of breathing

The Transition Ritual: Before entering any new environment, pause and notice three things you can see, hear, or feel

The Single Task Focus: For five minutes, do only one thing with complete attention—drink coffee, read an email, or walk to your car

The Present Moment Question: Regularly ask yourself, "What am I experiencing right now?"

Mindful Meeting Practices

Transform routine meetings into opportunities for present moment awareness:

The Arrival Practice: Spend the first minute of every meeting sitting quietly and becoming fully present before engaging

Active Listening Protocol:

- Give speakers your complete attention
- Notice your urge to formulate responses whilst they're talking
- Pause before responding to ensure you've truly heard them
- Ask clarifying questions to deepen understanding

The Energy Check: Regularly notice the emotional climate of meetings and how your presence affects it

Walking Meditation for Executives

Walking between meetings offers perfect opportunities for present moment practice:

Mindful Transitions: Walk deliberately between locations, noticing your feet touching the ground and the movement of your body

Nature Awareness: If possible, walk outside and notice natural elements—sky, trees, weather, sounds

Reset Walking: Use walks to transition between different types of thinking rather than continuing mental work

The Present Moment Approach to Common Leadership Challenges

Here's how present-moment awareness transforms typical executive situations:

Difficult Conversations

Traditional approach: Prepare extensively for every possible direction the conversation might take, and enter with anxiety about potential conflicts

Present moment approach: Prepare appropriately, then engage fully with what the person is saying and feeling in real-time

Benefits: More authentic connection, better understanding of underlying issues, creative solutions that emerge from genuine dialogue

Strategic Planning

Traditional approach: Spend most of the time projecting future scenarios and trying to predict outcomes

Present moment approach: Ground planning in a clear assessment of current reality, then use present moment thinking to develop flexible strategies.

Benefits: More realistic assessments, better contingency planning, strategies that adapt to changing conditions

Crisis Management

Traditional approach: Become reactive and scattered, trying to manage every aspect of the crisis simultaneously

Present moment approach: Stay calm and focused, address the most important elements first, and make decisions based on current information

Benefits: Clearer thinking under pressure, better resource allocation, more effective communication during crises

Building Your Present Moment Practice

Developing present-moment awareness is like building physical fitness—it requires consistent practice and gradual development.

Week 1-2: Foundation Building

Daily Practice:

- 5 minutes of focused breathing each morning
- Three micro-meditations throughout the day
- One mindful transition between activities

Focus: Simply noticing when your mind wanders without judging yourself

Week 3-4: Integration

Daily Practice:

- 10 minutes of morning mindfulness
- Mindful eating for one meal per day
- Present moment awareness during one meeting daily

Focus: Bringing awareness to routine activities

Week 5-8: Application

Daily Practice:

- 15 minutes of structured practice
- Mindful approach to one challenging situation daily

- Regular body awareness throughout the day

Focus: Using present moment awareness as a leadership tool

Ongoing Development

Daily Practice:

- Customised practice based on your schedule and needs
- Integration of mindfulness into leadership activities
- Regular retreats or intensive practice periods

Focus: Making present moment awareness your default mode of operation

The Present Moment Leadership Style

As you develop present moment awareness, your leadership style naturally evolves:

From Reactive to Responsive

Reactive leadership: Automatic responses based on past conditioning and future anxiety. **Responsive leadership**: Conscious choices based on current reality and clear thinking

From Scattered to Focused

Scattered leadership: Attention divided across multiple concerns, partial engagement with people and tasks

Focused leadership: Complete engagement with current priorities, full presence in interactions

From Anxious to Calm

Anxious leadership: Decisions driven by worry and stress, team anxiety increased by the leader's energy

Calm leadership: Decisions made from clarity and confidence, team stability increased by the leader's presence

From Controlling to Influential

Controlling leadership: Attempts to manage every variable through force and micromanagement

Influential leadership: Impact through quality of presence, authentic connection, and wise decision-making

Advanced Present Moment Practices

Once you've established basic present moment awareness, these advanced practices can deepen your capability:

The Observer Self

Learn to observe your own thinking and emotional patterns without being caught up in them:

- Notice thoughts arising and passing away
- Observe emotions without being controlled by them
- Witness your own reactions in real time
- Develop the capacity to choose responses rather than react automatically

Present Moment Problem Solving

Use present moment awareness to enhance your analytical capabilities:

- Fully define problems before jumping to solutions
- Notice assumptions and biases affecting your thinking
- Allow creative solutions to emerge through open awareness
- Balance analytical thinking with intuitive insights

Embodied Leadership

Develop awareness of how your physical presence affects your leadership:
- Notice your posture and how it influences your confidence
- Become aware of your breathing patterns during stress
- Use body awareness to gauge your emotional state
- Project calm and confidence through conscious physical presence

Measuring Progress in Present Moment Awareness

How do you know if your present-moment practice is working? Look for these indicators:

Subjective Measures

Increased calm: Less reactive to stressful situations, more emotional stability

Enhanced focus: Ability to concentrate fully on tasks and conversations

Better sleep: Less rumination means better sleep at night

Improved relationships: Deeper connections with colleagues, family, and friends

Greater satisfaction: More enjoyment from daily activities and achievements

Objective Measures

Decision quality: Better outcomes from choices made with present-moment awareness

Communication effectiveness: Feedback about your listening and responsiveness

Team performance: Improved results from teams when you're fully present

Stress indicators: Lower blood pressure, better health markers, reduced tension

Innovation metrics: More creative solutions and breakthrough thinking

Creating Organisational Cultures of Presence

Leaders who embody present moment awareness naturally create organisational cultures that value focus, authenticity, and mindful engagement.

Cultural Characteristics

Organisations led by present moment leaders demonstrate:

- **Reduced multi-tasking** and increased focus on priority activities
- **Better meeting quality** with more engagement and fewer distractions
- **Enhanced innovation** from space for creative thinking
- **Improved communication** with more listening and less reactivity
- **Lower stress levels** and higher employee satisfaction
- **Increased adaptability** from better awareness of changing conditions

Practical Implementation

Meeting protocols: Start meetings with brief centering, discourage devices, encourage full presence

Communication norms: Emphasise listening, thoughtful responses, and respectful dialogue

Decision-making processes: Include reflection time, encourage diverse perspectives, and avoid rushed judgements

Physical environment: Create spaces that support focus and calm thinking

Performance metrics: Include presence and mindfulness as leadership competencies

My Personal Journey with Present Moment Awareness

The shift from constant mental time travel to present moment awareness was perhaps the most transformative aspect of my recovery. It didn't happen overnight, and there were many moments when I reverted to old patterns of scattered thinking.

The Breakthrough Moment

The experience I described at the beginning of this chapter wasn't just a pleasant moment—it was a recognition that I had been living my entire adult life at a distance from my own experience. I realised that I hadn't truly tasted food, felt physical sensations, or been fully present in conversations for years.

This awareness was initially disturbing. How much life had I missed whilst mentally rehearsing future scenarios or replaying past events? But it quickly became exciting as I recognised the richness available in each moment.

The Ongoing Practice

Present moment awareness remains both my greatest tool and my ongoing challenge. During periods of high stress or significant change, I still notice my mind racing toward future scenarios or replaying past events.

The difference now is that I recognise these patterns quickly and have tools to return to present moment awareness. I have regular practices that anchor me in the here and now, and I've built present moment breaks into my daily schedule.

Most importantly, I've learned that presence isn't a destination—it's a continuous returning. Each moment offers an opportunity to come back to awareness, to engage fully with whatever is happening rather than what my mind thinks should be happening.

Common Myths About Present Moment Awareness

Let's address some misconceptions that prevent leaders from embracing present-moment practices:

Myth: "It's About Emptying Your Mind"

Reality: Present moment awareness is about focusing your mind, not emptying it. You're training your attention to engage fully with current experience rather than scattering across multiple time frames.

Myth: "It Makes You Passive or Complacent"

Reality: Present moment awareness increases your capacity for effective action by giving you access to complete information about current reality. It makes you more responsive, not less active.

Myth: "It Conflicts with Strategic Thinking"

Reality: Strategic thinking is enhanced by present moment awareness because it's based on a clear assessment of current conditions rather than anxious projections.

Myth: "It Takes Too Much Time"

Reality: Present moment awareness saves time by increasing focus and reducing the mental energy wasted on unproductive worry and distraction.

Myth: "It's Too 'Spiritual' for Business"

Reality: Present-moment awareness is a cognitive skill that enhances performance. Its benefits are measurable and practical, regardless of any philosophical or spiritual associations.

The Compound Effects of Present Moment Living

Like compound interest, the benefits of present-moment awareness accumulate over time:

Short-term Benefits (Days to Weeks)

- Reduced stress and anxiety
- Improved focus and concentration
- Better sleep quality
- Enhanced communication in meetings

Medium-term Benefits (Months)
- Better decision-making patterns
- Stronger relationships with colleagues
- Increased innovation and creativity
- Improved emotional regulation

Long-term Benefits (Years)
- Enhanced leadership effectiveness
- Greater life satisfaction and meaning
- Improved physical and mental health
- Wisdom and perspective that come from engaged living

Integration with Other Leadership Practices

Present moment awareness enhances rather than replaces other leadership skills:

Strategic Planning

Use present moment clarity to assess current reality accurately before projecting future scenarios.

Team Development

Be fully present during coaching conversations to understand what team members need.

Performance Management

Address performance issues with present-moment awareness rather than assumptions based on past patterns.

Innovation Leadership

Create space for breakthrough thinking by being present with challenges rather than immediately jumping to familiar solutions.

Chapter Summary: Key Takeaways

1. **Presence enhances performance**: Present moment awareness improves decision making, communication, and creative thinking.
2. **Attention is trainable**: Like physical fitness, the ability to stay present can be developed through consistent practice.
3. **Integration is key**: Present moment awareness works best when integrated into daily leadership activities rather than practised in isolation.
4. **Quality over quantity**: Brief moments of genuine presence are more valuable than lengthy periods of distracted meditation.
5. **Presence is contagious**: Leaders who embody present-moment awareness create cultures of focus and authentic engagement.
6. **Present awareness enables future success**: The quality of your future depends entirely on the quality of your present moment awareness and actions.

In our next chapter, we'll explore how to create lasting change by winning the mental game that determines all external success.

Chapter 9

Winning in Your Mind First - The Mental Game of Success

"Whether you think you can, or you think you can't—you're right."

— Henry Ford

The most important battle I ever fought wasn't in a boardroom, at a negotiation table, or during a crisis meeting. It was the daily battle that took place in my own mind between the voice that said "you're capable of handling this" and the voice that whispered "you're not good enough and everyone will find out."

For most of my career, I didn't realise this battle was even happening. I thought leadership was about external strategies, market positioning, and operational execution. What I discovered during my breakdown and recovery was that all external success is preceded by internal victory. You literally win or lose in your mind first, and then external reality follows.

This isn't positive thinking or wishful manifestation—it's about understanding how your internal narrative shapes your actions, which shape your results, which reinforce your internal narrative in an endless loop. When you learn to manage this loop consciously, you gain access to capabilities you didn't know you had.

The Internal Battlefield

Every morning when you wake up, before you check your phone or have your coffee, you step into a battlefield that exists entirely within your own consciousness. This battlefield is where your future is determined—not by the external circumstances you'll face, but by the mental stance you take towards them.

The Two Voices

Most high-achievers have two distinct internal voices:

The Achiever Voice:

- "I can figure this out"
- "I've handled challenges before"
- "This is an opportunity to grow"
- "I have valuable skills and experience"
- "I can learn what I need to know"

The Saboteur Voice:

- "I'm not qualified for this"
- "Everyone else is more capable than I am."
- "I'm going to fail and be exposed"
- "I don't deserve this success"
- "I'm fooling everyone about my abilities"

The voice that wins this internal dialogue determines:

- What opportunities do you pursue or avoid
- How you show up in important situations
- What risks you're willing to take
- How you interpret setbacks and failures
- Whether you persist through difficulties or give up

The Default Programming

Most people run on default mental programming installed during childhood and reinforced through years of experience. This programming operates automatically, below conscious awareness, and often conflicts with their conscious goals.

Common default programs for high-achievers include:
- "I must be perfect to be acceptable"
- "My worth depends on external achievement"
- "Failure means I'm fundamentally flawed"
- "I can't trust others to do things properly"
- "Success is temporary and will be taken away"

These programs run constantly in the background, influencing decisions and actions in ways that often sabotage the very success they're designed to create.

The Neuroscience of Mental Victory

Understanding what happens in your brain during mental conditioning can help you take conscious control of the process.

Neuroplasticity: Your Brain's Ability to Rewire

Your brain possesses a remarkable ability to form new neural pathways throughout your life. Every thought you have, every belief you hold, and every internal dialogue you engage in literally shapes the physical structure of your brain.

Repeated thoughts become neural highways: The more often you think a particular thought, the stronger and more automatic that neural pathway becomes.

New thoughts create new pathways: When you consciously choose different thoughts, you begin building new neural networks that can eventually become your default patterns.

Practice makes permanent: Just like physical skills, mental patterns become stronger and more automatic through repetition.

The Reticular Activating System (RAS)

Your RAS is a network of neurons that acts as a filter, determining what information gets your conscious attention and what gets ignored. It's programmed by your beliefs, expectations, and mental focus.

When your internal narrative is:

- "I'm not good enough" → Your RAS highlights evidence of your inadequacies
- "I can handle challenges" → Your RAS notices opportunities and resources
- "People are out to get me" → Your RAS focuses on potential threats
- "I'm supported and capable" → Your RAS recognises help and possibilities

The key insight: Your RAS doesn't determine what happens to you, but it does determine what you notice and therefore how you respond to what happens.

The Prefrontal Cortex: Your Mental Command Centre

Your prefrontal cortex is responsible for executive functions, including decision-making, planning, and emotional regulation.

When your internal narrative is positive and empowering, this region operates at full capacity. When your internal narrative is negative and limiting, its function becomes impaired.

Empowering narratives:
- Enhance cognitive flexibility
- Improve problem-solving ability
- Increase emotional regulation
- Support strategic thinking
- Enable creative solutions

Limiting narratives:
- Create cognitive rigidity
- Impair decision-making
- Increase emotional reactivity
- Reduce strategic capability
- Block creative thinking

Identifying Your Internal Narrative

Most people are unconscious of their internal narrative because it operates automatically. The first step in taking control is bringing these patterns into conscious awareness.

The Internal Dialogue Audit

For one week, pay attention to your internal commentary throughout the day. Notice:

Before important meetings or presentations:
- What do you tell yourself about likely outcomes?

- Do you rehearse success or failure scenarios?
- What assumptions do you make about others' reactions?

When facing challenges or setbacks:
- How do you interpret difficulties?
- What do you tell yourself about your ability to handle problems?
- Do you focus on solutions or obstacles?

After achievements or successes:
- How do you explain positive outcomes?
- Do you celebrate your contributions or downplay them?
- What do you predict about future challenges?

In relationships and interactions:
- What assumptions do you make about others' motivations?
- How do you interpret neutral or ambiguous interactions?
- What do you tell yourself about your value to others?

The Pattern Recognition Exercise

Look for recurring themes in your internal dialogue:

Competence Patterns:
- Do you generally trust your abilities or doubt them?
- How do you handle not knowing something?
- What's your default assumption about your capacity to learn?

Worth Patterns:
- Do you feel deserving of success and recognition?

- How comfortable are you with praise and achievement?
- What conditions do you place on your self-acceptance?

Control Patterns:
- How do you respond to uncertainty and change?
- What assumptions do you make about your influence over outcomes?
- How comfortable are you with delegating and trusting others?

Future Patterns:
- Do you generally expect positive or negative outcomes?
- How do you mentally rehearse upcoming challenges?
- What story do you tell yourself about your trajectory?

Rewriting Your Internal Operating System

Once you've identified limiting patterns, you can begin the process of conscious reprogramming.

The Identity Shift Process

Real change begins at the identity level—not just changing what you do but changing who you believe you are.

Current Identity: "I'm someone who struggles with confidence" **Target Identity**: "I'm someone who is growing in confidence every day"

Current Identity: "I'm not naturally good at public speaking" **Target Identity**: "I'm developing my communication skills and getting better with each opportunity"

Current Identity: "I'm too busy to take care of myself" **Target Identity**: "I'm someone who prioritises my wellbeing because it enables me to be better"

The key is making the new identity believable and actionable. Instead of jumping from "I'm terrible at this" to "I'm amazing at this," bridge the gap with "I'm learning and improving."

The Evidence Collection Practice

Your brain needs evidence to support new beliefs. Actively collect evidence for your desired identity:

Daily Evidence Gathering:

- What did I do today that demonstrates my target identity?
- What small progress did I make towards my goals?
- How did I handle challenges differently than I would have in the past?
- What feedback or recognition did I receive?

Weekly Pattern Review:

- What themes emerge from this week's evidence?
- How is my behaviour changing as my identity shifts?
- What additional evidence can I create next week?

Monthly Identity Assessment:

- How has my self-concept evolved this month?
- What old patterns am I successfully interrupting?
- What new patterns are becoming automatic?

The Internal Dialogue Intervention

When you notice limiting internal dialogue, use this intervention process:

Step 1: Pause and Recognise "I notice I'm telling myself [limiting story]"

Step 2: Question the Story "Is this thought helping me or limiting me?" "What evidence supports or contradicts this story?" "How would I advise a friend having this thought?"

Step 3: Reframe with a More Empowering Story "A more helpful way to think about this is..." "Instead of focusing on the problem, I can focus on..." "The opportunity in this situation is..."

Step 4: Align Action with New Story "Given this new perspective, what action would serve me best?" "How can I behave in a way that reinforces this better story?"

The Mental Rehearsal Advantage

Elite athletes use mental rehearsal to improve performance, and the same techniques can be applied to leadership challenges.

Visualisation for Leaders

Situation-Specific Rehearsal: Before important meetings, presentations, or difficult conversations:

- Visualise yourself handling the situation with confidence and skill
- Imagine positive but realistic outcomes
- Rehearse your responses to potential challenges
- See yourself remaining calm and resourceful under pressure

Identity-Based Visualisation:

- Imagine yourself fully embodying your target identity
- Visualise how this version of yourself would handle current challenges
- See yourself making decisions from a place of confidence and wisdom
- Imagine the impact this upgraded version would have on others

Outcome Visualisation:

- Clearly envision your desired professional and personal outcomes
- Make the visualisation specific and detailed
- Include the feelings associated with achieving these outcomes
- Regularly update and refine your vision as you grow

Mental Rehearsal Best Practices

Make it specific: Vague visualisations have little impact. Include specific details about how you'll think, feel, and behave.

Include obstacles: Rehearse overcoming realistic challenges rather than imagining everything going perfectly.

Engage all senses: The more vivid and multi-sensory your mental rehearsal, the more impact it has on your neurology.

Practice regularly: Like physical exercise, mental rehearsal works best when done consistently rather than sporadically.

Combine with action: Mental rehearsal enhances but doesn't replace actual practice and skill development.

Building Unshakeable Confidence

True confidence isn't the absence of doubt—it's the ability to take effective action in the presence of uncertainty.

The Confidence-Competence Loop

Traditional thinking: Competence → Confidence → Action → Results

Reality: Action → Results → Competence → Confidence

Most people wait to feel confident before taking action, but confidence comes from taking action and building evidence of your capability.

The Progressive Confidence Building Process

Level 1: Micro-Wins Start with small actions that are almost guaranteed to succeed:

- Have one difficult conversation you've been avoiding
- Complete one project you've been procrastinating on
- Take one small risk that frightens but doesn't overwhelm you

Level 2: Stretch Challenges Take on challenges that require some growth but are within reach:

- Volunteer for a project outside your comfort zone
- Apply for a role that requires new skills
- Start an initiative you care about but haven't prioritised

Level 3: Breakthrough Moments Pursue opportunities that represent significant growth:
- Take on a leadership role that intimidates you
- Start a business or major project
- Make a career change that aligns with your values

Each level builds evidence for your capability and expands your confidence to take on the next level.

The Failure Reframe

Confident people don't avoid failure—they reframe it as valuable data and a learning experience.

Traditional failure story: "I failed because I'm not good enough" **Confident failure story**: "I gathered valuable data about what doesn't work and I'm now smarter for next time"

Traditional failure story: "This proves I can't handle bigger challenges" **Confident failure story**: "This shows me what I need to develop to succeed at this level"

Traditional failure story: "I should have known better" **Confident failure story**: "I made the best decision I could with the information I had at the time"

The Internal Success Operating System

Successful people operate from a different set of internal assumptions than unsuccessful people. Here are the key components:

Growth Mindset vs. Fixed Mindset

Fixed Mindset: "My abilities are set and can't change significantly" **Growth Mindset**: "My abilities can be developed through effort and learning"

Leaders with growth mindsets:

- See challenges as opportunities to develop
- View effort as the path to mastery
- Learn from criticism and setbacks
- Find inspiration in others' success

Internal vs. External Locus of Control

External Locus: "My outcomes are determined by luck, circumstances, or other people" **Internal Locus**: "My outcomes are primarily determined by my choices and actions"

Leaders with an internal locus of control:

- Focus on their response rather than external circumstances
- Take responsibility for results without being paralysed by blame
- Invest energy in areas where they have influence
- Maintain agency even in difficult situations

Abundance vs. Scarcity Mentality

Scarcity Mentality: "There isn't enough success, recognition, or opportunity to go around" **Abundance Mentality**: "Success and opportunity can be created and shared"

Leaders with abundance mentality:

- Collaborate rather than compete unnecessarily
- Celebrate others' successes genuinely
- Look for win-win solutions in conflicts
- Invest in developing others without fear of being replaced

Advanced Mental Training Techniques

Once you've mastered the basics, these advanced techniques can deepen your mental conditioning:

The Future Self Dialogue

Regularly have imaginary conversations with your future self—the person you'll be in 5-10 years if you continue growing and developing:

- What advice would this future version give your current self?
- How would they approach your current challenges?
- What would they tell you to prioritise or change?
- What do they wish you understood about your current situation?

This technique helps you make decisions from wisdom rather than fear.

My Personal Mental Transformation

During one session, Christine asked me a question that changed everything: "John, what if you're exactly the right person for this challenge at this time in your life?"

The question stopped me cold because it was the opposite of everything, I'd been telling myself. As we explored this possibility, I began to see how my internal narrative had not been helping me in overcoming my challenges.

The Evidence Collection

As I began operating from this new mindset, I started collecting evidence that supported them:

- Challenges I handled better than expected
- Mistakes that led to better solutions
- Relationships that grew through investment of time and authenticity.
- Successes that felt earned rather than lucky

This evidence gradually convinced my subconscious that the new mindset was more accurate than the old one.

Organisational Applications

Leaders who master their internal game naturally create cultures where others can do the same.

Modelling Mental Mastery

When you demonstrate:

- **Calm under pressure** → Team members learn they can stay centred during challenges
- **Learning from failure** → Others become more willing to take appropriate risks
- **Growth mindset** → The organisation becomes more innovative and adaptable

- **Confidence without arrogance** → Team members develop their own quiet confidence

Creating Mentally Strong Cultures

Language matters: The words used in your organisation shape mental patterns

- Replace "failure" with "learning opportunity"
- Replace "problems" with "challenges" or "opportunities"
- Replace "we can't" with "how might we"
- Replace "that's not my job" with "how can I contribute"

Story matters: The stories told in your organisation reinforce mental patterns

- Celebrate growth and learning stories alongside achievement stories
- Share failure stories that led to breakthroughs
- Highlight examples of people overcoming mental barriers
- Recognise effort and process alongside results

Systems matter: Your organisational systems should support mental strength

- Performance reviews that include growth and learning metrics
- Recognition programmes that celebrate resilience and development
- Training programmes that include mental skills alongside technical skills

- Leadership development that addresses mindset and internal narrative

Measuring Mental Game Progress

How do you know if your mental training is working? Look for these indicators:

Internal Indicators

Thought patterns: Noticing more empowering thoughts and fewer limiting ones

Emotional regulation: Less reactivity to setbacks and more resilience during challenges

Self-talk: More supportive and encouraging internal dialogue

Confidence: Increased willingness to take on challenges and opportunities

Focus: Better ability to concentrate on what matters most

External Indicators

Decision quality: Making better choices under pressure

Leadership presence: Others note increased confidence and calm

Performance results: Improved outcomes in key areas

Relationship quality: Stronger connections with colleagues and team members

Innovation: More creative approaches to problems and opportunities

Behavioural Indicators

Risk-taking: Appropriate willingness to try new approaches

Feedback seeking: Actively requesting input and learning from it

Challenge acceptance: Volunteering for difficult assignments

Resilience: Bouncing back more quickly from setbacks

Growth actions: Consistently taking steps outside your comfort zone

The Compound Effect of Mental Mastery

Like compound interest, the benefits of winning in your mind first accumulate over time:

Short-term Effects (Weeks to Months)

- Reduced anxiety and increased calm
- Better decision-making under pressure
- Improved confidence in challenging situations
- Enhanced creativity and problem-solving

Medium-term Effects (Months to Years)

- Consistent high performance across different situations
- Stronger leadership presence and influence
- Better relationships and team dynamics
- Increased opportunities and career advancement

Long-term Effects (Years to Decades)

- Sustained success across multiple challenges and changes
- Deep sense of fulfilment and purpose
- Positive impact on others' development and success
- Legacy of empowering others to win in their minds first

Integration with Other Success Factors

Mental mastery enhances rather than replaces other success factors:

Skills and Knowledge

- Mental confidence allows you to apply your capabilities more effectively
- Growth mindset accelerates learning and skill development
- Internal strength supports you through the difficulty of mastering new competencies

Relationships and Networks

- Authentic confidence makes you more attractive as a colleague and leader
- Mental abundance helps you build genuine connections rather than transactional relationships
- Internal security allows you to be vulnerable and create deeper trust

Strategic Thinking

- Clear internal narrative supports better strategic decision-making
- Mental calm allows you to see patterns and opportunities others miss
- Confidence enables you to pursue bold strategies when appropriate

Chapter Summary: Key Takeaways

1. **Internal precedes external**: All external success is determined by internal mental patterns and narratives.
2. **Awareness enables choice**: You can't change mental patterns you're not aware of—consciousness is the first step.
3. **Identity drives behaviour**: Changing what you do permanently requires changing who you believe you are.
4. **Evidence builds belief**: Your brain needs proof to support new mental programmes—actively collect evidence for empowering beliefs.
5. **Practice makes permanent**: Mental patterns become stronger through repetition—conscious practice rewires your brain.
6. **Failure is data**: Reframing setbacks as learning opportunities builds antifragile confidence.
7. **Mental mastery is contagious**: Leaders who win in their minds first create cultures where others can do the same.

In our final chapter, we'll explore how to move beyond simply being "OK" and step into a life of growth, purpose, and authentic success.

Chapter 10
What if OK Wasn't OK?

"The cave you fear to enter holds the treasure you seek."

— Joseph Campbell

Life is filled with moments when we tell ourselves, "I'm fine." "Everything's OK." We've all been there. It's a quick fix, a way of smoothing over discomfort, hiding vulnerability, or avoiding the uncomfortable truth that something inside us is unsettled. But what if, just for a moment, we consider the idea that "OK" may not actually be OK at all?

What if the familiar, comfortable "OK" is actually a facade? A distraction from deeper feelings, unresolved pain, or unspoken desires? What if settling for "OK" means we're missing out on living our fullest, most authentic lives?

The "OK" Trap: A False Sense of Safety

We live in a world where external appearances are often given more weight than internal truths. The phrase "I'm OK" has become a socially accepted answer to questions about our emotional or mental state. But what happens when we say it and don't really mean it? The danger of constantly telling ourselves or others that everything is "fine" is that it can lead us into a state of complacency.

Complacency is the silent killer of personal growth and happiness. It lulls us into a sense of comfort, where we believe we're doing all right even when we're not. But by accepting "OK" as the baseline, we suppress the possibility of exploring what could be better, what could be different, or what could be more fulfilling.

Consider this: if we never acknowledge that we're not truly "OK," we don't give ourselves the chance to address the root causes of our discomfort. We become stuck in a loop where "OK" becomes the enemy of progress, and we stop striving for more meaningful changes. What if, instead of constantly pushing through with "OK," we stopped to assess whether we are truly happy, fulfilled, and at peace?

The Facade of Perfection: Living in a Society of Filters

In today's world, we are constantly bombarded with the polished lives of others—through social media, advertising, and even in our personal interactions. Everything looks perfect, edited, and curated. It's easy to fall into the trap of comparing our behind-the-scenes to everyone else's highlight reel. As a result, we often feel the pressure to present a life that's "OK"—even if it's not.

But when does this filtered version of life become a problem? When does pretending that everything is OK prevent us from being honest with ourselves and others? The danger lies in the constant need for validation, the idea that "OK" equals success, and that the absence of turmoil means we've figured it all out.

However, this is rarely the case. Most of us are navigating some form of struggle, some deep inner conflict that we feel the need to suppress to keep up appearances. But by not confronting our reality—by glossing over the messiness of life with a façade of

"OK"—we miss the opportunity for genuine connection and healing.

The Truth Beneath the Surface: Honouring Our Feelings

It's vital to take a step back and acknowledge our true feelings. What if "OK" isn't really OK at all? What if we've become so accustomed to the idea of pretending everything is fine that we've lost touch with what it truly means to feel alive and authentic?

Honouring our feelings means acknowledging discomfort, sadness, fear, anger, or any other emotion that might come up, without shame or judgment. It's about giving ourselves permission to feel, instead of constantly putting on a mask of contentment. If we are ever going to break free from the "OK" trap, we must learn to express ourselves openly and embrace vulnerability.

The power of naming our feelings and being present with them is transformative. When we give ourselves permission to say, "I'm not OK," it's an invitation for healing and growth. It is in the discomfort of not being OK that we find the opportunity to create change, to grow, and to cultivate a deeper connection with ourselves and others.

The Perils of Avoidance: Why We Run from Our Feelings

In the face of uncertainty, discomfort, or pain, it's common to try to avoid those feelings. Whether it's through distractions like work, social media, or even substance use, the goal is often to silence the uncomfortable truth that we're not OK. But avoidance does nothing but delay the inevitable.

If we continue to push aside our true feelings, we create emotional and mental blockages. These blockages can manifest in a variety of ways: chronic stress, anxiety, depression, or even physical symptoms. The longer we avoid addressing the truth—that we are not "OK"—the harder it becomes to move forward.

What if we reframed the idea of "OK" as a moment of opportunity? Instead of running from discomfort, we could lean into it, knowing that it is in the acknowledgement of our struggles that healing begins. If we constantly hide behind the mask of "OK," we rob ourselves of the chance to confront our truth and make positive changes.

Turning "OK" into a Springboard for Growth

The truth is, no one is always "OK." We all have our moments of doubt, confusion, and pain. But here's the powerful thing: these moments can serve as catalysts for change. When we stop pretending that everything is fine, we open the door to transformation.

Rather than seeing "OK" as the end goal, we can shift our mindset to see it as the beginning of something much greater. If we're not OK, it's a sign that we need to act, to take a closer look at our lives and our emotional health, and to make the necessary adjustments to move forward.

Turning "OK" into an opportunity for growth begins with being honest with ourselves. It means taking a hard look at our lives and saying, "What can I do to feel better? To be more aligned with my true self?" It could be seeking therapy, setting boundaries, making a career change, or even just allowing ourselves to rest. Whatever the path is, it starts with acknowledging that "OK" isn't enough and that we deserve more.

The idea of "OK" doesn't have to be a one-size-fits-all response to life's challenges. Instead of viewing "OK" as a place of complacency, we can redefine it as the starting point for growth and healing. By acknowledging that "OK" might not always be enough, we give ourselves the space to grow, to heal, and to live more authentically. And in doing so, we free ourselves from the pressure to always appear fine, allowing us to embrace the messy, beautiful reality of life.

The next time someone asks how you're doing, take a moment to reflect. Is everything really "OK"? If not, maybe that's where your journey of transformation begins.

There are so many people living their lives thinking ok is good enough. I wouldn't want anyone to go through some of the experiences I have had over the last 18 months, and I wish I had been able to pick this book up long ago.

The things we have covered, I have done and still do, and I want to help you lead and live a better life. One with more internal peace and one where you have the skills required to manage inner turbulence.

You don't have to be in therapy to benefit from this book. It is for anyone who wants to grow and understand how their mind works and how they can manage how they think. It is therapy on its own. The book shows that people who others think are strong, determined, driven and successful have the same challenges as anyone else. We hope that this topic becomes part of education so that people are equipped with the skills for their life ahead.

I hope you have enjoyed reading it and that it will sit on your desk or bedside table as something to keep referring to.

I wish you success and remember, if you follow the process, the results will look after themselves.

The Butterfly's Promise: Your Transformation Awaits

As we conclude this final chapter and this journey together, I want to return to the butterfly that has guided us throughout this book. The butterfly's message is both simple and profound: transformation is not only possible—it's your natural destiny.

You may be reading this from your own cocoon stage—that dark, uncertain period where everything familiar seems to be dissolving. Or you may be in the early stages of emergence, feeling new capabilities stirring within you but not yet ready to trust your wings. Wherever you are in this process, know that you are exactly where you need to be.

The caterpillar entering its cocoon has no guarantee of what will emerge. It operates purely on instinct, on the deep knowing that surrender is necessary for transformation. You too must trust this process, even when you can't see the outcome.

Your breakdown—whether it was a dramatic crisis like mine or a quiet recognition that "OK" wasn't enough—is not your failure. It's your invitation to become who you were always meant to be. The struggles you've faced, the limitations you've acknowledged, the help you've sought—all of it has been preparing you for this transformation.

Like the butterfly, you will emerge not as an improved version of who you were, but as someone entirely new. You will possess capabilities you never imagined—authentic leadership, deep resilience, genuine compassion, and the ability to help others through their own transformations.

The world needs leaders who have walked through the darkness and emerged transformed. It needs executives who recognise that true strength is born of vulnerability, that real power lies in service, and that lasting success grows from genuine connection with others.

Your flight—the expression of your transformed self in the world—will inspire others to believe that their own transformation is possible. Every time you choose growth over comfort, authenticity over facade, connection over control, you give others permission to do the same.

The butterfly doesn't fly to prove anything or achieve anything—it flies because flight is now its nature. When you complete your transformation, authentic leadership won't be something you do—it will be who you are.

So spread your wings. Trust your new capabilities. Embrace your authentic power. The world has been waiting for the leader you're becoming.

Your metamorphosis is complete. It's time to fly.

I wish you success and remember, if you follow the process, the results will look after themselves.

But most importantly, remember this: you are not just OK. You are capable of extraordinary things. You deserve more than just getting by. You have the power to create a life of meaning, purpose, and authentic success.

The choice, as always, is yours.

What will you choose?

Printed in Dunstable, United Kingdom

72831905R00117